ROAD LOCOMOTIVES AND TRACTORS

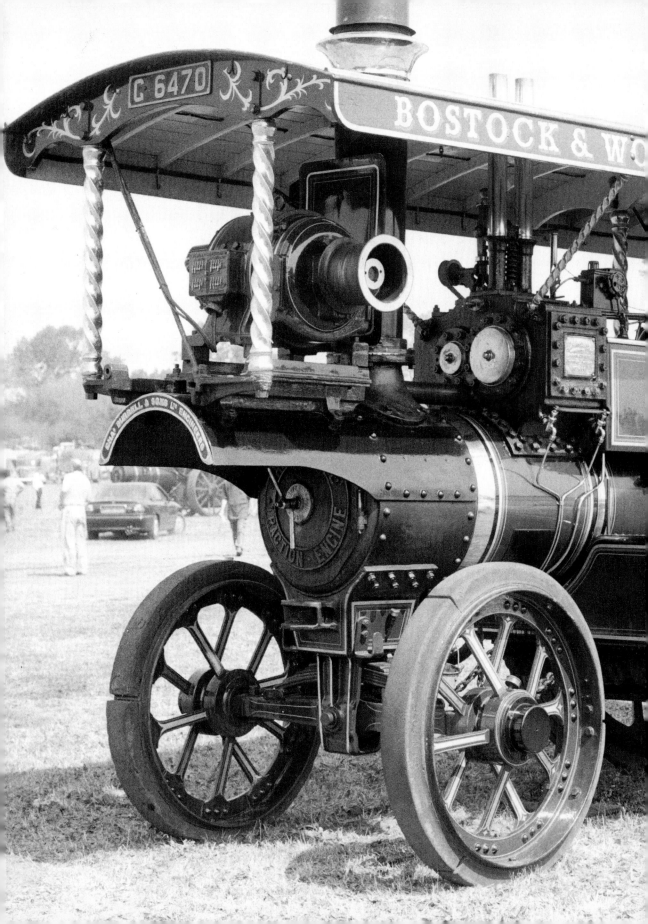

ROAD LOCOMOTIVES
AND TRACTORS

FROM THE GOLDEN AGE OF STEAM POWER

ERIC SAWFORD

SUTTON PUBLISHING

First published in 1999 by
Sutton Publishing Limited · Phoenix Mill
Thrupp · Stroud · Gloucestershire · GL5 2BU

British Library Cataloguing in Publication Data
A catalogue record for this book is available from the British Library.

ISBN 0-7509-2113-7

Frontispiece: This magnificently restored Burrell showman's road locomotive, no. 3669 *Nero*, together with its sister engine *Rajah*, toured the length and breadth of the country with the famous Bostock & Wombwell Travelling Menagerie.

™ ALAN SUTTON™ and SUTTON™ are the trade marks of Sutton Publishing Limited

Typeset in 10/12 pt Palatino.
Typesetting and origination by
Sutton Publishing Limited.
Printed in Great Britain by
Butler & Tanner, Frome, Somerset.

Contents

Introduction   vii

1. Showmen's Road Locomotives   xiv

2. Showmen's Tractors   72

3. Road Locomotives   86

4. Steam Tractors   142

For many visitors to the Great Dorset Steam Fair the line-up of showmen's road locomotives, set against a background of vintage fairground rides, proves the greatest attraction. Showmen's engines travel considerable distances to be present at this event. Nearest the camera is the Wallis & Steevens tractor *Royal Star*, built in 1914, which was owned by Goodey Brothers of Twyford where it was used to haul a set of gallopers. Next in line is Burrell no. 3555, *The Busy Bee*, and alongside no. 3669 *Nero*.

A very popular event is one of the Frank Lythgoe showmen's engines hauling five or six more around the ring. The sheer length and turning circle means the engines are seldom seen in a straight line, as in this picture of Burrell no. 3093 *Dreadnought* in action.

Introduction

Many years have passed since showmen's road locomotives were regularly used to haul fairground rides around the countryside, providing power for the rides on site. I can remember Thurston's engines passing through Huntingdon High Street on their way to the next fairground with several heavily loaded wagons in tow. Unfortunately, this was long before I became involved in photography, but it is something I will always remember, as I do the sight, smell and sounds the engines made as they gently rocked to and fro generating power. It is, of course, still possible to enjoy this experience at a great many events. The Great Dorset Steam Fair is unquestionably the most spectacular, especially after dark, boasting a variety of vintage rides in all their glory in a splendid setting. The kaleidoscope of colours, and fairground equipment working to capacity, draws thousands of visitors to view and enjoy the wide range of attractions.

Burrells of Thetford were very highly regarded for their showmen's road locomotives, but they did not have the market to themselves as several other companies also built this type of engine. Fowlers of Leeds and Fosters of Lincoln both produced excellent, powerful designs. Fodens, Garretts and Brown & May were other companies that also produced road locomotives but on a much smaller scale, and only one example from these three companies has survived into preservation: the Garrett, like so many other showmen's engines, started life as a road locomotive before working the fairgrounds.

It was by no means unusual for engines to start their working life on general haulage work, later to be purchased and converted to full showman's specification. A small number of such conversions eventually proved unsuitable for various reasons, and were laid up or returned to haulage work. As steam started to be replaced on the fairgrounds many fine showmen's engines were put to work on agricultural duties, usually with the dynamo and twisted brass removed but still retaining the canopy. Had this not happened a considerable number of those in preservation today would not be with us, having long since fallen victim to the scrapman's cutting torch.

By the end of the nineteenth century Burrells were constructing road locomotives especially for showland use; some of these early engines were not fitted with full-length canopies and had little or no twisted brass. During this period and for a number of years afterwards they had straked wheels which gave a very bumpy ride compared with later examples with solid rubber tyres. Handling these engines required considerable skill and judgement, as road surfaces were often rutted, dry and dusty in summer. Roads in towns and cities were usually stone sets, which was fine if the weather was favourable but could be treacherous in wet or icy conditions. Moreover, availability of coal and water, narrow roads, tight turns, pot-holes, hills and access to fairgrounds all had to be taken into consideration, especially with the heavily loaded wagons. The engine crews were mostly old hands who had travelled the roads for many years and were well aware of particularly difficult stretches of road. Showmen's road locomotives were called upon to haul loads of up to eight trailers of varying sizes, and as can well be imagined it was necessary to take

These two showmen's engines are currently preserved many miles apart: on the left is *Island Chief* from Scarborough, and on the right *Western Pioneer* from Aberdeen. The latter, which many readers may know better as *Teresa*, was on one of its infrequent journeys south of the border from its home base.

Burrell road locomotive no. 3047 *Lord Roberts* heads a timber haulage demonstration in the rolling Dorset countryside, in conjunction with the well-known Fowler crane engine no. 17212 *Wolverhampton Wanderer* minus crane jib. *Lord Roberts* is an example of Burrells' contractors' engines which were more heavily constructed than normal.

things very carefully on down gradients to prevent runaways. Over the years some mishaps did occur. On arrival at the site the showmen would immediately start to assemble the rides.

Travelling with any road locomotive was testing for the engine crew, but heavy haulage could present even bigger problems. Setting out with a very heavy, outsize load required very detailed planning. Weak bridges, narrow twisting lanes, and steep gradients had to be avoided, and once under way, obstacles such as road signs, lights and overhanging trees had to be negotiated or perhaps even removed where possible, and replaced once the load was safely past. Particularly heavy and awkward loads were often handled by three engines, two in front and another at the rear. Fowlers of Leeds built many fine road locomotives especially suited to this work, with the class B6 'Super Lions' being their ultimate design. One of the most famous is no. 17105 *Atlas*, which has survived into preservation. The Norman Box Company was among the leaders in the haulage of large, difficult, outsize loads, operating a number of large Fowlers with many Herculean loads to their credit. Some of the large road engines were fitted with cranes to facilitate unloading on arrival, especially with bulky items such as Lancashire boilers. The crane jib towered above the front of the engine, causing the crews additional problems, especially when working through built-up areas. Luckily several examples have survived into preservation.

Several other engine builders were involved with the construction of road locomotives. Burrells and McLarens were among the market leaders, with other firms constructing small numbers. With their experience in building showmen's engines, Burrells were highly regarded, and they built many fine engines for general haulage work, a few of which were fitted with cranes. A number of later-type Burrells have survived to this day. One survivor is no. 3197, built in 1910, which was supplied new to Screen Brothers of Oldbury, Birmingham, and worked until 1958. This engine had a particularly hard working life, especially during the First World War when it was in use twenty-four hours a day with two engine crews. Surprisingly, it retained its original livery, appearing on the rally field well into the 1990s. Burrells also built road engines of heavier construction, known as contractors' engines. One excellent example is no. 3057 *Lord Roberts*, built in 1908, which spent its working life hauling boilers, timber and bricks.

The superbly restored Burrell road locomotive no. 4000 *Ex Mayor* heads a line-up of showmen's engines built by Burrell and Fosters of Lincoln, who were also highly regarded for their powerful road locomotives.

Nine years separate construction of these two superb examples of Burrells showmen's road locomotives. Nearest the camera is *Nero*, built in 1915, which travelled throughout the British Isles. *Earl Haig* was completed at Thetford nine years later, travelling in the west country for a Gloucester-based showland operator. Both engines ended their working days on agricultural work before being rescued for preservation.

One very fortunate road locomotive was the Garrett 6 nhp no. 27946 *Vera*, which was built in 1909 and sold to J. Harkness of Belfast; in use until 1967 it passed straight into preservation.

In November 1901 Aveling & Porter completed no. 4885, a splendid 8 nhp type LC8 road locomotive for use in Chatham Dockyard. This engine was constructed to an Admiralty specification that included two water columns and two pressure gauges, and a capstan fitted to the rear axle. This engine was later to pass into the ownership of the well-known East Anglian engine dealers G. Thurlow & Sons of Stowmarket, and was converted to showman's specification for Charles Presland. In the 1970s it was seen at a few local events in East Anglia. Sold in 1980 at the famous Holywell sale it went first to Lancashire and then on to a new owner in Lincolnshire, where it remains.

One Fowler road engine which appears at various events during the year, including the Great Dorset Steam Fair, is no. 15649 *Providence*, a splendid example of the A9 class road locomotives. Built in 1920, *Providence* worked until 1955 on timber and general haulage. In December 1966 it hit the headlines when it ran from York to Ravenglass hauling a new 15-inch gauge locomotive destined for the Ravenglass & Eskdale Railway. Crossing the Pennines in December could not have been very comfortable for the enginemen.

Towards the end of the nineteenth century the Army realized the capabilities of road locomotives for hauling guns and supplies, work previously done by pack animals. The engines were more than capable of handling the loads, but there was little or no

Most of the leading companies built road locomotives for heavy and general haulage work, as well as tractors for handling lighter loads. Nearest the camera is Burrell road locomotive no. 3941 *The Badger*, alongside a magnificently restored example of a tractor built by Fosters of Lincoln.

protection for the engine crews. In 1900 Fowlers received an order for four armoured road trains for use in South Africa in the Boer War. These trains certainly offered protection but what conditions on board must have been like for the crews, even on trials in this country, can only be imagined, let alone in the heat of South Africa. The armour plating weighed 4.5 tons and restricted visibility considerably. Noise and heat were just two of the problems. Many other types of haulage engine were used in South Africa. Road locomotives were also used in India, especially on the North-West Frontier.

During the First World War the British Army used huge numbers of engines and wagons in France and Belgium. After the war most of these were included in the army surplus sales and many passed into private hands. The condition of items offered for sale varied enormously, from almost new to virtually worn out, and all stages in between. This flooding of the market naturally created considerable problems for the engine building companies for several years.

From the late nineteenth century there had been a demand for engines of all types in many parts of the world. The leading engine companies were well aware of this potential market, and as a result many engines, including considerable numbers of road locomotives, were sent overseas, and some of them have survived. Fowlers' type TE2 haulage and winding engines, which carried a wire rope drum mounted under the boiler, were particularly popular in Russia, and a considerable number were ordered for.export. However, before the contract was completed circumstances changed and the balance were sold to the home market; several of these have survived into preservation.

Heavy haulage demonstrations are a regular feature at the Great Dorset Steam Fair, where engines have to work hard on the climb up to the back of the site. Here two powerful Fowler road locomotives head the load: the leading engine is no. 17105 *Atlas*, followed by no. 17106 *Duke of York*, with Burrell *Lord Roberts* bringing up the rear.

The somewhat solemn face on the front of this railway locomotive fits well the indignity of being hauled around the countryside on a trailer, albeit with steam power. The engine had been loaned by the Swanage Railway for a special event, and for most of the journey it was hauled by powerful road locomotives. The picture is included here as it shows details of the heavy wagon, with the Burrell *Lord Roberts* assisting at the rear.

Haulage work which did not require heavy road locomotives was carried out by steam tractors, which were designed in many cases to be operated by one man. These tractors were widely used on local delivery work, such as furniture removal, hauling produce to market from farms and gardens, and many similar duties, while many large houses and estates owned small 3 nhp engines, used principally to convey coal and other bulky materials to and from the railway station. Most of the engine building companies were involved in this market, and often gave type names to their designs. Many soon became widely known, including Burrells' 'Gold Medal' tractor, Garretts' '4CD', Fowlers' 'Tiger', Fosters' 'Wellington', Taskers' 'Little Giant' and so on. A few steam tractors were also purchased by showmen, fitted with a dynamo, lighting and a canopy and used for lighter loads. Steam tractors are widely sought after by enthusiasts as they offer many advantages.

As steam power was replaced on the roads many engines were sold for agricultural use, once-proud showmen's engines among them. In most cases the dynamos and twisted brasswork was removed, though the canopy was usually retained to offer protection. As the wind of change swept through the farming industry and internal combustion tractors became widely available, steam engines were laid aside, although a few soldiered on, being used principally on drainage work. In the 1950s it was not uncommon to see derelict engines that had been simply abandoned in farmyards, fields and contractors' yards; others found their way into scrapyards or were cut up on site. Enthusiasts rescued some of these fine engines and in the early days most required little effort to restore them to working order. Any that needed new boilers, fireboxes or major repairs were at that time widely regarded as being beyond restoration. Engines in poor condition changed hands for what today seem ridiculous figures, but in many cases their owners were only too pleased to see the back of them, years of exposure to the elements, often without any protection, having taken their toll. In the very early rally days engines appeared very much as they were when they finished work, with showmen's engines still in road locomotive form, and others with perhaps just a coat of paint. Despite the interest many very interesting examples were still being cut up, especially 'tractions', and a number of notable survivors disappeared at this time.

In more recent times even hopelessly derelict examples have been rescued, requiring new boilers, fireboxes and sometimes a complete rebuild. Many had lost numerous parts over the years, especially the brass and copper fittings. Nowadays, replacement of major items is commonplace, albeit costly, and it is essential to ensure that those in preservation are kept in working order.

Some of the engines which were present at events in the 1950s and 1960s have vanished from public view, placed in storage to await engineering work. Others have become static exhibits in museums, still on public display but not in steam. At the time of writing (1998) a number of showmen's road locomotives are undergoing a major rebuild, including some which have not steamed for many years, and a few may well reappear in public very soon. There are still in existence some showmen's engines which have never been rallied and on which no restoration work has commenced; these generally require extensive rebuilds and replacement parts to restore them to working order. It is hoped that they too will one day make their rally debut.

In the forty-plus years since the preservation movement started countless engines have changed hands, some more than once. With this in mind I have selected for inclusion in this title some pictures from the 1960s, when the engines looked very different. I have also included pictures of engines in action in the 1960s, which have since become museum exhibits.

During the heyday of the road locomotives, most showmen took great pride in their engines, keeping them in immaculate condition with highly polished brasswork. There were a few which carried little or no twisted brass and title lettering, although they did have a dynamo fitted for providing power to the rides. Throughout the country the arrival of the fair was something to look forward to, with the major events attracting huge crowds. For the larger gatherings engines would arrive from all directions and could hardly fail to be noticed, the sight of the polished road locomotive hauling the road train was itself a good advertisement for the fair. Engines would be hard at work all around the fair.

When engine rallies started in the 1950s no one could have guessed just how these events were to grow over the years, or how many fine engines of numerous types were to end up in preservation. Indeed the variety to be seen at rallies today is a fitting tribute to the design and engineering work of the engine builders of the day.

1. Showmen's Road Locomotives

The showmen's road locomotives, with their gleaming paint and brasswork highlighted by coloured bulbs, are unquestionably the most glamorous of all types of road engines in preservation. These powerful engines were constructed by several companies, and a considerable number of designs were built over the years. Burrells of Thetford produced the highest number and, as might be expected, have

the most survivors. Fowlers of Leeds and Fosters of Lincoln were also highly regarded for their road engines. These three were the market leaders, but several other companies also built a few examples for showland service and fortunately some of these have survived. Only the leading showmen could afford to purchase new engines; others might buy one which had spent its first few years on general haulage work and have it converted to showman's specification, while a few would buy an engine that had already been in showland service for some time, use it until a major overhaul was required and then lay it aside or maybe pass it on for agricultural service. Looking at these magnificent showmen's road locomotives today, it is very difficult to visualize the condition that most were in before being rescued for preservation: many were just rusting hulks, stripped of all their brasswork, and their moving parts seized solid after years of exposure to the elements. Such is the dedication of steam enthusiasts that many examples which not so long ago were thought to be beyond restoration have been carefully rebuilt to their former glory.

As a company, Aveling & Porter were more concerned with steamrollers – hardly surprising as they were the market leaders, with buoyant home and export sales. They also constructed traction engines, tractors, wagons and road locomotives, some of the later examples of the latter being built as crane engines. Only three Aveling & Porter road locomotives are in preservation in Britain, the earliest being an LC6 design built in 1900. This fine LC8 class 8 nhp two-speed road locomotive, *Samson*, was built in 1901 as works no. 4885. It was a special order from the Admiralty for use at Chatham Dockyard, the specification calling for two water columns and pressure gauges and a capstan fitted to the rear axle. In due course the engine was purchased by G. Thurlow & Sons of Stowmarket. It was converted to showman's specification for Charles Presland, remaining in his ownership until 1946. *Samson* spent its final working years on agricultural work in Suffolk.

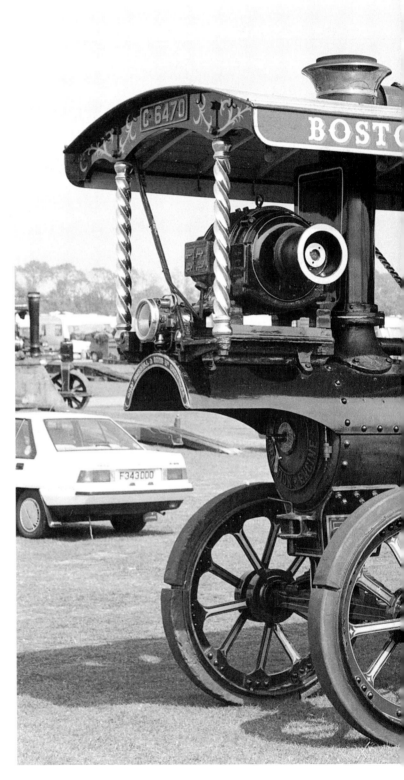

Rajah and *Nero*, the two 5 nhp showmen's road locomotives owned by Bostock & Wombwells, have the distinction of being the most widely travelled showmen's engines. No. 3669 *Nero* was built in 1915 and is a superb example of the company's 'Devonshire' type. Its sister engine *Rajah* is currently preserved in Devon. In 1998 these two engines were seen together at a Cornish rally. In their working days neither engine was particularly decorative, with only a few twisted canopy pillars and little else in the way of brasswork. They also had only a few lights, as their principal use was to provide power to the menagerie.

The west country showmen Anderton & Rowland were well known for their stud of Burrell showmen's road locomotives. The last to arrive was 'Scenic' type no. 3912 *Dragon*, supplied new in 1921, and heavily embellished with brasswork which included swaged boiler bands and brass stars. The engine was originally supplied on straked wheels, but these were later replaced with new solid rubber tyres. Its relatively small rear wheels were a distinct advantage on the hills of the west country.

(Opposite, top) Burrell no. 3288 *Nancy* was widely thought to be beyond restoration after forty years' exposure to the elements but such was the determination of its owners that *Nancy* has been restored to this fine condition, after many hours of painstaking work – to say nothing of the expense. Built in 1911, *Nancy* was supplied new to J. Manders of Mile End, London, to haul and power a set of steam yachts. During the First World War it was commandeered by the government and worked on general road haulage for the Dartmoor China Clay Company. In 1921 it was sold to Joseph Brewer, a showman based at Indian Queens in Cornwall, to work with his gallopers. After just seven years the Burrell was laid up. Forty years later it was purchased for preservation, but it was to be many years more before it made its rally debut.

(Opposite, bottom) *Dragon* is certainly no newcomer to the rally scene. It is seen here in the 1960s complete with an illuminated nameboard. To this day *Dragon* still travels under its own steam to many local events.

A considerable part of Burrell's income was derived from engines supplied to travelling showmen. They were market leaders in this field, and constructed more examples of this type of engine than any other company over a forty-year period. Many showmen's road locomotives were supplied on straked wheels, as seen on no. 2072 *The Masterpiece*. This is one of the oldest surviving Burrell showmen's road locomotives. Built in 1898, it was supplied to John Cole Amusements of Bristol, where it remained throughout its working life. During the war, however, it was used on more mundane duties.

This 7 nhp Burrell, no. 3159 *The Gladiator*, spent its working life in the west country. Initially with Anderton & Rowland, to whom it was supplied new, from 1932 it was in the ownership of T. Whitelegg & Sons of Plymouth. It worked until 1941 when it was laid up in their yard at Exeter.

(Opposite, top) Burrell no. 3890 *Majestic* was completed at Thetford in March 1921 and supplied to J.H. Herbert of Southampton, where it was to remain until 1952, doing very little work after 1940. It has had several owners in preservation and is currently based in Hampshire.

(Opposite, bottom) Another Burrell showman's locomotive that was very familiar in the west country during its working days was no. 3887 *The Prince of Wales*. This 8 nhp 'Scenic' was built in 1922 and supplied to Henry Jennings & Sons of Devizes, hauling and providing power to their Whales Scenic Ride.

When this picture of 8 nhp Burrell no. 2625 *Lady Pride of England* was taken it was still in the process of restoration. Built in 1904, it was to have several showland owners, the first being W. Buckland of Buckingham. In preservation it has had even more.

(Opposite, top) Burrell 8 nhp no. 2894 *Pride of Worcester* made a welcome reappearance on the rally fields in 1996 following an extensive rebuild. Built in 1907, it was supplied to Henry Strickland & Son of Worcester, later passing to Arnold Brothers, based at Cowes on the Isle of Wight, who renamed it *Edward VIII*. It was later owned by E.J. Harris of Hook, Surrey. In 1948 it was sold for scrap to Hardwicks of Ewell but fortunately it was rescued by Miss Sally Beech; renamed *Lord Fisher*, it worked with a set of gallopers. Without Miss Beech's intervention this Burrell may well have been lost.

(Opposite, bottom) A number of showmen's road locomotives started life on general haulage, and this was the case with Burrell 6 nhp no. 3979. Built in 1924, it was supplied new to W.J. Taylor & Sons Ltd of Midsomer Norton, Somerset. In later life it passed into the ownership of Mrs F. Symonds of Gloucester and was converted to full showman's specification carrying the name *Earl Haig*. After its showland days were over it spent its last few years on agricultural work. It eventually became derelict and slowly sank into the ground, so much so that getting it out was to prove no easy task.

For a number of years Burrell no. 3878 *Island Chief* was missing from the rally scene, but it is currently back in Yorkshire where it started work, having had several owners during preservation. Built in 1921, this 6 nhp engine was supplied to Robert Payne of Beverley, Yorkshire, carrying the name *Excelsior*. It then passed to Arnold Brothers of Cowes, Isle of Wight, who renamed it *Island Chief*. During the 1960s this engine was preserved in north Norfolk and was one of several showmen's road locomotives present at the Raynham Day event held near Fakenham.

Burrell 'Scenic' no. 3884 *Gladiator* in action at Ickleton in 1961, having been recently overhauled. Also present was Burrell showman's engine no. 3118 *Dreadnought*, at that time still in road locomotive form without a canopy and dynamo.

Burrell 5 nhp no. 3926 *Margaret* was built in 1922 and supplied to Henry Thurston of Northampton. In recent years it has been in preservation in Holland carrying the nameplate *Margaret* on one side, *Stokomolief* on the other. It has now returned to this country.

This splendid 8 nhp Burrell showman's engine, no. 3334 *The Bailie*, was completed in September 1911. It was to have three showland owners: G. Green of Glasgow had it for three years before selling it on to H. Bradley, who kept it until 1931; subsequently it came south of the border to Silcock Brothers, based in Warrington. *The Bailie* remained with them until 1958 when it was purchased for preservation. It has been with the present owner for over forty years and over the years it has visited a great many events covering a wide area.

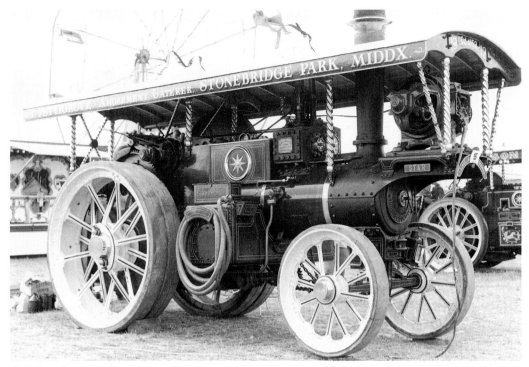

Another showman's engine to start its working life as a road locomotive was 7 nhp no. 3423 *Star*. Built in 1912, it was supplied to T.C. Greensmith & Co., Burton-on-Trent. In 1919 it was sold to Hereford Brick Company, and in the mid-1920s it went to Tom Pettigrove and was converted to showman's specification by Openshaws and named *Star*. In 1938 it was laid aside at Stonebridge Park where it remained for forty-five years. The elements took their toll and it took ten years of restoration to bring this fine engine back to working order.

Burrells were highly respected for a great many years for their powerful showmen's road locomotives. No. 3865 *No. 1* was built in 1920 and was bought by the well-known Midlands showman Pat Collins. It was during his ownership that the engine was converted to the 'Scenic' type.

Many of the principal engine building companies exhibited their latest engines at the annual Royal Shows. The Burrell stand in 1924 included 5 nhp road locomotive no. 3950 *Progress*, which was completed at the St Nicholas Works on 27 March 1924, finished in lake/red livery. After the show it was supplied to A. Cox & Sons Ltd of Abingdon, Oxfordshire, and used on general haulage. It was later sold to Swindon-based showmen R. Edwards & Son and converted to full showman's specification. It was last used by them at the end of the 1936 season after which it remained in store for fifty-one years.

Another Burrell road locomotive to be converted to full showman's specification while in the ownership of R. Edwards & Sons was no. 3651 *Earl Kitchener*. Built in 1915, it was used on heavy haulage by its first owners, E. Hill & Sons, also of Swindon. This engine spent much of its working life travelling the west country fairs, and was sold by its showland owners in 1986.

(Opposite, top) Built in 1909, Burrell 6 nhp no. 3090 *Fermoy* was supplied to Birmingham-based showmen Pool & Bosco. In 1921 it was sold via a dealer to Mrs Shepherd who kept it for six years before selling it on, after which it was used on agricultural work. For nearly forty years it has been based at Charminster, Dorset.

(Opposite, bottom) One Burrell showman's road locomotive still in the process of restoration is no. 2547 *Endurance*, built in 1903. It is on the left in this Great Dorset line-up but is not in steam. It started life on general haulage for J.K. Cooper & Sons, haulage contractors of Maidenhead, later moving to Charles Prior of Braywick, also in Berkshire. In 1933 it was sold to M. Stokes, a Basingstoke-based showman, and was converted to showman's specification by Wallis & Steevens. The engine on the right is the Brown & May *General Buller*.

The Bristol-based showmen Anderton & Rowland had a number of Burrell showmen's engines, five of which have survived into preservation. One of these, no. 3443 *Lord Nelson* worked for them until 1940 when it was sold to another Bristol showman, W. Coles. It was used for only a short time before being laid up. For a number of years *Lord Nelson* was owned by the National Motor Museum at Beaulieu, changing hands in the mid-1990s.

(Opposite, top) There are only a small number of Burrell showmen's engines older than this one in working order. This splendid 8 nhp example, no. 2668 *Britannia*, was built in 1904 and supplied new to H. & W. Thurston, Cambridge. During its working life with this family it travelled with a set of dodgems. Its last showland owner was Mr A. Manning of Stevenage, Hertfordshire.

(Opposite, bottom) The Burrell showman's engine no. 2701 *Black Prince* has been a static exhibit at Bressingham Steam Museum for many years. During the 1960s it was to be seen at a number of local events including the 1963 Raynham Day where this picture was taken. Built in 1904 as a road locomotive and supplied new to J.W. Harris of Hook Norton, Oxfordshire, in 1915 it moved on to J. Hickey & Sons of Richmond where it remained for twenty years. It was then purchased by Fred Gray, a Hampstead-based showman, and converted. During the Second World War it was used on demolition work in London. In 1945 *Black Prince* was sold to H. Goodey of Twyford before ending up at Hardwicks of Ewell, from where it was rescued for preservation in 1962.

The massive scenic railway fairground rides introduced in the early 1900s led to the development of the 'Scenic' engine design. These engines were equipped with two dynamos, the one behind the chimney being used to excite the field coils of the main unit. This system offered greater control when starting the ride and better acceleration and speed during operation. Set against the attractive backdrop of Stanford Hall, this is Burrell 'Scenic' no. 3938 *Quo Vadis*. It was built in 1922 for William Wilson of Peckham, London, and travelled with his Rodeo Dragon Car Switchback. In 1940 it was purchased by Wall Brothers who used it for fifteen years. Eventually it was sold to Hardwicks from where it was rescued for preservation. *Quo Vadis* has had several owners since then, including one in Northern Ireland, and is now with another new owner in Dorset.

No. 2804 *The Griffin* is another of the surviving Burrell showmen's road locomotives which was owned by Anderton & Rowland from 1923 to 1930. Built in 1906 for Alf Payne of York and named *White Rose* it was to have five showland owners, including Pat Collins who named it *The Griffin*.

(Opposite, top) The Burrell 'Scenic' *Gladiator* pictured at Raynham in 1963. This fine engine was often seen in East Anglia at this time. It was completed on 14 March 1921, and supplied to its new owner, Fred Gray of Hampstead, carrying the name *Wonder*. This was changed to its present name during its showland days. The engine was sold for preservation in 1955, and its home is now at Exmouth, Devon.

(Opposite, bottom) For many years this fine Burrell 'Scenic' engine, no. 3610 *William V*, was a familiar sight at events in the Home Counties and Midlands. Built in 1914 for Wm Murphy of Newcastle upon Tyne, it travelled with a set of scenic motors. During its working life it had two more owners in the north of England before going south to Kent-based showmen J. Bottom & Sons. Some readers may recall this engine more recently in preservation in Scotland carrying the name *Flower of Scotland*.

This may not be a brilliant picture technically but this was a very rare opportunity to photograph Burrell 8 nhp 'Scenic' no. 3827 *Victory* in steam at a rally in the early 1960s. Completed in May 1920, this engine was supplied to Charles Thurston of Norwich. *Victory* is part of the famous Thursford Collection.

(Opposite) Burrell 'Scenic' no. 3886 *Lord Lascelles* ready for the day's events. Note the many features on this fine engine: polished brasswork, a dynamo and wide drivebelt, a fine set of lamps and the brass plates carrying the builder's name. Note the legend on the front of the canopy, 'Pride of Them All'; the lettering on the side of the canopy in the engine's working days read 'H. Grays Steam Yachts'. This engine was used for eighteen years in London and the Home Counties before being laid up in Grays' yard at Mitcham, where it was to remain for twelve years. It was purchased in 1951 by Jack Hardwick, who brought it back into working condition; renamed *Tulyar*, it took part in a Coronation pageant in 1953. It changed hands again later that year.

Burrell 7 nhp showman's road locomotive *Lightning II* has the distinction of being the only one of this type to leave the works in green livery. It was supplied new to Emmerson & Hazard of Whitehaven, Cumbria in 1913. In 1955 it was purchased by its present owners R. Preston & Son and used to start the haulage business of this well-known company. *Lightning II* was last used on heavy haulage two years later. This is an engine that always attracts attention due to its smart green livery which it has carried since new.

No. 3444 *His Lordship* is one of several 8 nhp Burrell showmen's road locomotives to have survived into preservation. Built in 1913, it was supplied new to George Green of Glasgow, transferring in 1915 to John Green. In 1935 it was sold to Silcocks of Warrington who used it until 1947 and it was purchased for preservation two years later. *His Lordship* has travelled extensively in the British Isles during preservation. Note the decorations on the belly tanks.

Twenty 'Scenic' showmen's road locomotives were produced by Burrells, eleven of which have survived into preservation. These engines were designed to work with the massive scenic railway rides introduced in about 1910. No. 3888 *General Gough* was supplied new to S. Bolesworth & Son of Leytonstone, London, and was one of the last showmen's engines to be used on the fairgrounds. This splendid engine was found in a disused gravel pit in Oxfordshire and rescued for preservation. It is pictured below in the famous showmen's line-up, one of the major attractions of the Great Dorset Steam Fair.

No. 3847 *Princess Marina* was built in 1920 and supplied to Miss Hannah Parkin of Ipswich. It was later sold to John Barker & Sons in the same area. Most of this 6 nhp Burrell showman's working life was spent on East Anglian fairgrounds, and it is pictured below against the background of fairground rides at the Great Dorset, with its power-cables coupled up.

Burrell 'Scenic' no. 3909 was built in 1922 and was named *Pride of the Road* when it was supplied new to A. Holland of Swadlincote, Derbyshire. It was renamed *Winston Churchill* in preservation.

(Opposite, top) Several showmen's engines carry the name *Dreadnought*. No. 3118 started life as a road locomotive for McCreath & Co. of Berwick-on-Tweed. In 1925 it was sold to C. Abbott of Norwich, and during its fifteen years with this owner it travelled with a cakewalk and chair-o'-planes until it was sold on for general haulage. In its last few working years it saw commercial service with three different owners.

(Opposite, bottom) Burrell 'Scenic' no. 3285 *King George V* was built in 1911, going new to Abbot & Barker of Norwich, and later moving to Swales Forest, based at Dartford, Kent. The brass plate below the dynamo reads Mather & Platt Manchester. The lettering 'Continental Scenic Railway' on the side of the canopy is the exact wording it carried for part of its showland days.

This 5 nhp 'Devonshire' type showman's road locomotive spent its early showland days touring Cumberland and south-west Scotland in the ownership of Taylor Brothers of Workington. Built in 1914, no. 3555 *The Busy Bee* was supplied with no twisted brass or a dynamo. It was commandeered for war work in the First World War and was used on timber haulage at Thirsk & Elizah Charnley Town End Sawmills at Ulverston and also in the Windermere and Ambleside areas. After the war it was returned to Taylor Brothers, and travelled with several different rides including a steam motor switchback, gallopers and finally dodgems until 1940 when sold for agricultural work. It had two more owners before being rescued by Dr J.L. Middlemiss for preservation.

Another showman's road locomotive with a long and varied history is Burrell no. 3489 *King George VI*. Built in 1913, it started life as a road locomotive in the ownership of Ponsford & Sons of Topham, Devon, later being sold to E.T. Padfield of Shepton Mallet. In 1919 it was sold again, this time to the boiler-makers J. Hickey, where it carried the name *City of London*. It was not until 1936 that it entered showland service for Swales Bolsworth of Dagenham. This career was short-lived, and just two years later it was sold to E. Andrews of Tunbridge Wells, finishing its fairground days in 1948. *King George VI* was purchased for preservation in 1950, and in due course it became the first showman's engine to attend a steam rally.

Burrell 6 nhp road locomotive no. 3343 was supplied new to Ralph Dumma of Jedbergh with the rather unusual name *Jetharts Here*. Built in October 1911, it was to remain on general haulage duties until it was converted to showman's specification for H. Stocks of Ipswich in 1922 when it was renamed *Princess Mary*. It was laid up in 1939.

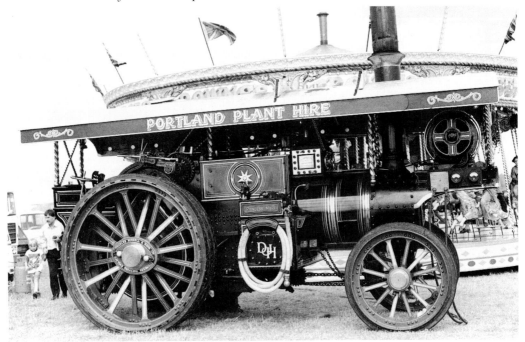

Several names recur among preserved showmen's road locomotives, one of them being *Princess Mary*. This is Burrell no. 3949. Built in 1923, it was exhibited at the Smithfield Show. Its first owner was William Nichols of Forest Gate. This engine was built with a lower canopy than usual so it could negotiate very low bridges in parts of London. Later in its working life it was bought by Charles Presland of Tilbury. *Princess Mary* was a familiar sight at London fairs for over thirty years.

No. 3933, a 7 nhp engine, was completed in April 1922 in special plum-coloured livery for J. Anderton & Son of Plymouth. This is one of two preserved showmen's engines carrying the name *Princess Mary* and currently with owners in East Anglia.

This is no. 3933 *Princess Mary* photographed over thirty years ago in Norfolk, the county in which it is preserved. Prior to the change-over to diesel power, large fairs would have several showmen's engines present, attracting onlookers as they generated power for the rides.

The 'Special Scenic' was the ultimate Burrell design. Twenty of these powerful engines were built, eleven of which still survive. One of the finest examples is no. 3483 *Perseverance the Second*, built in 1913 and supplied to Harniess Brothers of Swinton, Yorkshire. It remained there until 1944 when it was bought by Mrs Cole of Chichester, Sussex, who used it for two years. It was sold for preservation in 1953. At the back of the engine can be seen the crane used for unloading trailers, and building up and dismantling the ride.

Burrell no. 4000 *Ex Mayor* was completed in February 1925 and finished in Great Eastern blue for G.T. Tuby & Sons of Doncaster. Mr Tuby held a number of civic positions, which was reflected in the names given to his showmen's engines: *The Councillor, The Leader, The Alderman, The Mayor* and *Ex Mayor*. All were built by Burrells. *Ex Mayor* has had several owners in preservation. It is pictured (above) at an early Expo held on the East of England Showground when preserved at Henley-on-Thames. The lower picture shows the engine as it is now.

Burrell no. 3093 *Dreadnought*. Built in 1909, this 8 nhp engine was supplied new to Arthur Holland of Swadlincote with whom it spent its entire working life. In 1925, while still in Arthur Holland's ownership, the engine was returned to the company's works at Thetford for a major overhaul. At the same time the opportunity was taken to fit a crane tower on to the coal bunker. The top photograph shows the engine some years ago when it was in the ownership of W. Dorman. Note the pram near the front wheels. The bottom photograph shows *Dreadnought* as it is today, as part of the Frank Lythgoe collection.

Completed at Thetford in 1909 and finished in a crimson/yellow livery, *Dreadnought* was to spend its entire working life with one owner, travelling the London fairgrounds until it was laid up in 1942. It is pictured here in full cry hauling six full-size showmen's engines around the ring. This is a very popular attraction with rally visitors, offering as it does the opportunity to hear and see an engine working hard.

Some engines retained the same name throughout their working life while others had several, as is the case with Burrell no. 4030 *Dolphin*. Its first owner was Wm S. Davies of Stoke-on-Trent where it was named *The Dolphin*. It was later purchased by J. Shaw of Sheffield and renamed *The Guvnor*. The name changed again when the engine was in the ownership of H.J. Wallis of Seaforth, this time to *The Commando*.

(Opposite, top) Burrell 6 nhp no. 3295 *Princess Royal* photographed in 1962 when it was in preservation at Saffron Walden. Built as a road locomotive in 1911, it was supplied new to Wm Elworthy of Crosslands, Tiverton, Devon. Ten years later it entered showland service for A. Adlem of Freemantle, Hampshire, later passing to R. Gilliam. *Princess Royal* has had several owners in preservation, including one in Ireland. For some years now it has been in Japan.

(Opposite, bottom) Burrell 7 nhp no. 2879 *Princess Royal* started its working life for Henry Thurston, and over the years it travelled with several different rides, including a scenic railway and later scenic motors, and finally with Thurston's son's Noah's Ark. In 1932 it was sold to F. Harris of Pulborough, being finally laid up in 1948. Over the years it has had three different names, the other two being *Sweet Nothing* and *Lord Nelson*.

This unusual picture of Burrell 7 nhp no. 3871 *Teresa* clearly shows details of the controls, bunker and rear wheels. It is currently preserved in Aberdeen and makes only occasional visits south of the border. Built in 1921, *Teresa* was supplied new to Sidney Stock of Ipswich and travelled the Eastern Counties. Later it was sold to Hardiman & Strong of Bristol where it was named *Pioneer*. Moving on to John Cole it became *Western Pioneer*, the name which can be seen under the dynamo.

For a number of years Burrell 'Scenic' no. 3886 *Lord Lascelles* was a familiar sight in East Anglia and further afield in the ownership of the late Steve Neville, often travelling to and from events under its own steam. When he purchased this fine engine in 1964 it was in a dismantled state and required a lot of work, including a new firebox shell, before it could be steamed again. The lower picture shows *Lord Lascelles* as it appears today. This is one of the finest examples of the 'Scenic' engines in preservation. Built in 1921, it was supplied in lake/yellow livery to Henry Gray of Hampstead Heath. Following the outbreak of the Second World War it was laid up and remained in their Mitchem yard until purchased for preservation.

In the early 1920s several of the finest Burrell showmen's locomotives that have survived into preservation were completed at Thetford. No. 3890 *Majestic* was among them, being completed in March 1922 for J.H. Herbert, based at that time in Southampton. It remained with the company until 1952, but like so many engines it was little used following the outbreak of the war.

(Opposite, top) Another Burrell to start its working life on general haulage was no. 3651 *Earl Kitchener*, built in 1915 and supplied new to E. Hill & Sons of Swindon. Eight years later it passed into the ownership of R. Edwards & Son, also of Swindon. It was converted to full showman's specification and remained with the Edwards family until 1986.

(Opposite, bottom) This picture of no. 3651 *Earl Kitchener* was taken at the Great Dorset Steam Fair and shows clearly the very ornate flywheel decoration. This engine has had three owners in preservation.

Fowler 10 nhp B6 class no. 19783 *King Carnival II* was built in 1932 for F. McConville of West Hartlepool, County Durham. In 1941 it was requisitioned by the government, stripped of its showland fittings and used on general haulage. After two owners it was sold in 1951 to the boiler-makers John Thompson of Wolverhampton and was used by them until 1968 when it was purchased for preservation.

(Opposite, top) This showman's road locomotive, Fowler's 'Supreme' no. 20223, was completed in 1934 and went new to Mrs A. Deakin & Sons of Brecon. The engine was a special order with left-hand steering and chrome fittings. As with *King Carnival II* it was requisitioned for heavy haulage at the outbreak of the war. In due course it ended up at Hardwick's scrapyard from where it was rescued for preservation.

(Opposite, bottom) One of the best-known Fowler showmen's engines is no. 15657 *The Iron Maiden*, made famous by its appearance on cinema and television screens. Built in 1920 as a road locomotive, its early years were spent on stone haulage in the ownership of Portland Stone Quarries, Dorset. It was later bought by Mrs H. Oadley of Derbyshire and converted to showman's specification, carrying the name *Kitchener*.

Several of the Fowler showmen's engines in preservation today started life on general haulage, being purchased by showmen after a few years and converted to full showman's specification. This was the case with 7 nhp R3 class no. 15319 *Queen Mary* which started life with the Portland Stone Quarries in Dorset. Just nine years after it left Leeds it was converted by Eddisons of Dorchester for Richard Townsend & Sons of Weymouth.

(Opposite, top) Fowler R1 class showman's road locomotive no. 9393 *Sir John Fowler* was completed in March 1904. Its showland owners were J. Rawlings and J. Noyce & Sons. In preservation this engine has appeared in black livery as well as the more familiar maroon.

(Opposite, bottom) Fowler A8 road locomotive no. 13922 *Girly* started its working life on general haulage, and two years later it was converted to showman's specification by Openshaws of Reading. During its showland days it was owned by John Hoadley of Gateshead and later by Slators Amusements of Carlisle. Shortly afterwards it was laid up due to the outbreak of the Second World War.

54

Fowler 10 nhp B class no. 14425 *Carry On* was completed in 1916 and commandeered by the War Department to tow heavy artillery in France. After the war it was converted to showman's specification by Openshaws of Reading and sold to Codonas of Scotland. In 1943 it was bought by McGiverns of Northern Ireland, working there until 1958. It returned to England in 1961.

Carry On photographed at the Ickleton Rally in 1962. Since then this fine engine has been in preservation at Redbourn, Hertfordshire, and for the last few years at Stotfold.

As already mentioned, there are a number of showmen's road locomotives which carry the name *Dreadnought*. This example is Fowler 7 nhp A5 class no. 11108. Built in 1909, part of this engine's working life was spent travelling with Coles' Venetian Gondolas.

These two powerful showmen's road locomotives were built by different companies. Nearest the camera is Fowler no. 11108 *Dreadnought*, built in 1909, and alongside is Burrell 'Scenic' no. 3886 *Lord Lascelles*, built in 1921.

Two consecutively numbered 10 nhp
Fowlers showmen's locomotives are in
preservation, no. 14424 and no. 14425
Carry On (see page 56). These engines
weigh in at almost 20 tons each. No.
14424 *Valiant* is not usually seen far from
its base at Bedford. This B class engine
was built in 1916. It is pictured here in
the pleasant surroundings of Old
Warden. At one time it was well known
in the Midlands, travelling for Pat
Collins and carrying the name
Dreadnought.

Fowler no. 14424 *Valiant*, pictured in 1962 when it carried the name *Goliath*, the nameplate being mounted just below the dynamo at this time.

(Opposite, top) The big Fowler road locomotives were ideal for heavy gun haulage during the First World War. No. 14862 *Evening Star* was built in 1917 and is a fine example of the R3 class 8 nhp design. After the war the engine was used on heavy haulage work. In the early 1920s it was rebuilt by Fowlers as a three-speed showman's road locomotive and sold to Jacob Studt of South Wales.

(Opposite, bottom) John Murphy of Gateshead, County Durham, placed a special order with Fowlers for two 8 nhp R3 class showmen's road locomotives, which were completed in May 1920. No. 15652 *Repulse* seen here travelled with sister engine *Renown* working Murphy's Proud Scenic Peacock ride. During the early war years both engines were used on timber work in North Yorkshire.

On rare occasions it is possible to see *Repulse* and *Renown* standing side by side as they would have done so many times during their long showland life. Note the legends on the front of the canopies: on *Repulse*, 'Mighty in War & Peace', and on *Renown*, 'Plain but Powerful'.

(Opposite, top) The second of the two Fowlers, no. 15653 *Renown*. Note the Thompson-Watson feast crane at the rear of the engine which was used for handling the cars of the ride. This engine has travelled extensively in Britain and Europe while in preservation.

(Opposite, bottom) Fowler R3 class no. 15117 *Headway* was built as a road locomotive in 1920 and sold to J. Drury & Son of Laceby, Lincolnshire, who used it on heavy haulage work for six years. It was then purchased by Nottingham-based showman Morney Mellors, converted to showman's specification and travelled with a set of gallopers. In 1930 Mellors joined J.W. Hibble to become Hibble & Mellors, and the engine remained with them until the late 1940s.

In this line-up of showmen's engines are examples built by Fowler, Foden and Burrells. All have gleaming brasswork, coloured lights and immaculate paintwork.

(Opposite, top) This powerful 10 nhp McLaren was supplied to the War Department in 1917 for hauling guns in France. After the war it was sold to Midlands-based showman Pat Collins, converted to full showman's specification and named *Goliath*. It is now part of the Frank Lythgoe collection.

(Opposite, bottom) This is the sole surviving Garrett showman's road locomotive no. 27160 *Crimson Lady*, photographed after it changed hands in 1991. This engine started its working life on general haulage, being converted to showman's specification when it was bought by Thomas Sheppard of Wellingborough, travelling with a set of gallopers. In 1935 it changed hands again, ending its working days on agricultural duties. It is shown here in crimson livery, shortly after it arrived in Huntingdon from its previous home in Essex. Within a short time work began on dismantling the Garrett, the first stage of a lengthy rebuilding project which is due for completion in 1999.

In this picture the Garrett no. 27160 is carrying its original name, *British Hero*, and is nearing completion after a long overhaul that included new boiler-barrel, firebox, chimney and rubber tyres. The engine will be repainted in green livery.

(Opposite, top) Fodens are best known for their steam wagons but in their early days they also built traction and road locomotives, including ten showmen's. Only one of the latter has survived into preservation. No. 2104 *Prospector* was completed in March 1910 and supplied new to W. Shaw & Sons of Sheffield where it remained for its entire working life.

(Opposite, bottom) Another very rare showman's engine is the sole surviving Brown & May, no. 8742 *General Buller*, built in 1912. This was the last of its type to be built by the company before it closed just over a year later. Supplied new to Cook's of North Wales, it worked with a set of gallopers, later passing to Mellor Brothers of Nottingham. *General Buller*'s final working years were on agricultural duties.

Foster 7 nhp no. 14502 *Victory* was completed in August 1920 and supplied to Mrs C. Bird of Watford. It travelled with her rides for many years until it was sold in 1943 to Flanagan Brothers. After lying disused for a time it was eventually rescued for preservation.

(Opposite) Fosters of Lincoln were highly regarded for their showmen's and road locomotives. No. 14153 *Admiral Beatty* started life as a road engine, but in 1921 it was purchased by Henry Thurston and converted to showman's specification. As with so many other once-proud engines, it ended its working life on agricultural duties. During its fairground days with Thurstons it became well known at many East Anglian fairs. For a number of years *Admiral Beatty* was part of a collection of engines owned by the late Tom Paisley; during this time it was seen at a number of events, mainly in East Anglia. It was sold at the famous October 1980 auction sale which attracted buyers and enthusiasts from both Britain and overseas.

Also completed in August 1920 was Foster 7 nhp no. 14501 *Victorious*. This engine spent its entire working life with the Pettigrove family of Stonebridge Park, Middlesex. It was used to haul and power a set of Tidman three-a-breast gallopers. It was eventually laid up for forty years at Chadwell Hill before being purchased for preservation.

(Opposite, top) Seven showmen's engines built by Foster survive, although not all are in working order. No. 14632 *Success* is a fine example of the 10 nhp design. It was built in 1934 and sold new to Hibble & Mellor, working until 1942 when it was sold to Hardwick's of Ewell for scrap. It was bought in the mid-1950s by Darby's Sand & Gravel of Sutton and used for five years on agricultural work until sold for preservation.

(Opposite, bottom) This splendid 10 nhp Foster showman's engine, no. 14446 *The Leader*, was completed in October 1921. It was to become one of the engines owned by the well-known Midlands showman Pat Collins. There are seven Foster showmen's engines in preservation, only two of which are of the 10 nhp design. A 6 nhp example, no. 3200 *Aquitania*, is expected to make its return to the rally fields in 1999 after many years' absence.

2. Showmen's Tractors

In the days before diesel units were available, showmen relied entirely on steam power. The powerful majestic showmen's road locomotives took care of the heaviest loads, often hauling as many as eight fully laden trailers. Showmen's tractors were used to haul lighter loads around the countryside and,

once on site, to provide power. Just like their larger cousins, the showmen's tractors had the usual dynamo and twisted brasswork; some showmen who wanted their tractors to be every bit as bright and attractive as their road locomotives covered them with brasswork. As with their larger cousins, many entered showland service after a few years of general haulage work. Most of the surviving fairground tractors were built by Burrells and Garretts.

Several of the surviving Burrell 'Gold Medal' tractors started their working lives on general haulage duties, later being purchased by showmen and converted. This splendid Burrell 'Gold Medal' tractor, no. 3192 *St Bernard*, started life as a crane engine for the War Department in 1910. After the First World War it passed into the ownership of a Southampton-based showman, J.H. Herbert. This tractor has been in preservation for a great many years. Burrell no. 3191, which also started life with the War Department in 1910, still survives.

Burrell no. 3433 *Peter Pan* was completed at Thetford in December 1912 and exhibited at the Smithfield Show as a conventional 'Gold Medal' tractor. It was sold to G. Kemp & Co. of Aldershot where it was principally used for timber haulage. It was later sold to showland owner Mrs J. Cole of Chichester where it remained until 1950.

(Opposite) This Burrell tractor, no. 3453 *The May*, was supplied new to W. Sedgewick of Oldham for use with their 'American Jungle' show. After a period of several years it returned to showland, this time in the ownership of J. Downs. Note the decorated flywheel. This splendid 'Gold Medal' tractor can often be seen with the owner's set of gallopers; in the lower picture it is shown at an event held at the North Norfolk Railway.

Burrell no. 3497 *May Queen* was built in 1913, going new to T.A. Everton of Droitwich, Worcestershire. During the First World War it was commandeered for war service. It was subsequently purchased by W. Beach for showland use, for a while carrying the name *Conqueror* but later reverting to its old name. It finished work in 1950, becoming the last tractor in showland use. It remained with the Beach family until 1952.

(Opposite, top) *Reliance*, works no. 2876, started its working life at Thomas Park's Guildford Park Brick, Tile & Pottery Works in Guildford in 1907. Later it was sold to Petersfield-based showmen Wall Brothers, although it had not been fully converted to showman's specification. In its early days the Burrell was named *Little Samson*.

(Opposite, bottom) Burrell no. 2876 *Reliance* was laid up in 1943 by its showland owners Wall Brothers.

Burrell no. 3786 *Sunny South* was completed in June 1918 and supplied to E. Longhurst & Son of Epsom, Surrey, carrying the name *Tiger*. It was later converted to showman's specification for J. Beach and used on the fairgrounds from the mid-1930s.

(Opposite, top) Foster 4 nhp tractor no. 13036 *Pride of Essex* started life on general haulage work. It was later purchased by a Kent-based showman travelling in the southern counties.

(Opposite, bottom) This Foster 4 nhp 'Wellington' tractor, no. 14066 *Endeavour*, was built in 1915, and it had several showland owners, among them J. Beach of Sunbury-on-Thames and B. Ayres of Uxbridge. It is preserved in Lincolnshire and is seen at many events during the year.

Garretts of Leiston completed works no. 33358 *Lord George* in October 1918 and supplied it to the War Department. In 1921 it was converted to a showman's tractor for Fred Harris, travelling with a set of gallopers. It remained with Fred Harris until 1953 when it was rescued for preservation. Although derelict, it was complete except for the dynamo; even the brasswork was intact.

(Opposite, top) Still in the process of an overhaul, Garrett no. 33358 *Lord George* pictured at Chrishall Grange in 1984.

(Opposite, bottom) Garrett no. 32122 *The Greyhound* was built in 1914, and during its showland service it travelled in London and the Home Counties with the Beach family. Tractors were responsible for hauling lighter loads.

Originally ordered by the War Department as a crane engine but later cancelled, Garrett no. 33486 *Queen of Great Britain* was completed in April 1919. It was sold to Browning Brothers, haulage contractors based in Gloucestershire. In 1921 it was purchased by the Bristol-based amusement caterers W. & J. Cole and converted for showland use, travelling the west country fairs with a set of gallopers.

(Opposite, top) Garretts completed 4CD no. 33284 in October 1918 as a standard tractor in green livery. It was supplied to the Ipswich Haulage Company, but just three years later it was returned to the Garrett works, converted to a showman's tractor, named *Princess Maud* and supplied to Wm Abbott, an Ipswich-based showman. In 1943 it changed hands, going to the Edmonton-based showman W.A. Greenway.

(Opposite, bottom) This Wallis & Steevens oil-bath tractor, no. 7482 *Royal Star*, was completed in December 1914 and was requisitioned for service by the War Office. It then enjoyed a short career on the fairgrounds, hauling a set of gallopers for Goodey Brothers of Twyford. It ended its working days on stone haulage, before being laid aside. It became derelict, but after forty years it was rescued for preservation.

3. Road Locomotives

Anyone who witnessed massive road locomotives hauling heavy, bulky and often outsized loads is unlikely to forget the spectacle and sounds they made, especially when they were working hard. Over difficult terrain it was not unusual to have two engines at the front and another at the rear. Fowlers of Leeds built many magnificent examples for heavy haulage, as did a number of other leading companies. Moving a large load over long distances required careful planning, with engines and crews often being away from home for weeks. The route itself had to be chosen with care in order to avoid weak bridges etc., while poor road

surfaces were another consideration. Almost certainly somewhere along the route obstacles would have to be moved due to the sheer size of the load and total length of the road train. Water and coal would need to be supplied along the route, and would be consumed in quantity on a long journey. Other road locomotives were used on a much more local basis, delivering bricks, road stone, boilers and all manner of heavy loads. Some were regularly used to haul materials from railway stations, goods traffic being plentiful in those days. We are lucky today that a wide variety of engines are in preservation. Some, such as the big Fowler 10 nhp *Atlas*, worked on some of the heaviest loads throughout the British Isles. Others, their owners' pride and joy, were in daily use, quietly going about their business, vital to the smooth running of the owners' work.

No. 8471 *Clyde*, a fine example of the Aveling & Porter 6 nhp class YLD road locomotive, was completed in December 1914. It was supplied to S. Frampton of Farnham where it was used on general haulage and later worked in Cornwall. In preservation it has had several owners. Only a very small number of road locomotives built by this company have survived into preservation. They include two of this type, both three-speed compounds built in 1914 and 1920 respectively.

Burrell no. 2789 *The President* was built as a showman's road locomotive and supplied new to G.H. Kemp of Leicester in 1905, carrying the name *Lord Kitchener*. Two years later it was converted to a road locomotive and used for heavy and general haulage. (It was usually the other way round, with showmen buying and converting former road locomotives.) It was to have two more owners in its working life before being laid aside in 1953. It is seen here in 1961 prior to being sold to Bressingham Steam Museum, where it has been a static exhibit for many years. Note the showman's brasswork still on the engine.

(Opposite, top) Burrell no. 3593 *Duke of Kent* was completed at Thetford in June 1914. Its first owner was C. Tassell of Luton, Chatham, Kent, where it was employed on general haulage work. Five years later it was purchased by Scotts Sawmills of Chatham, who used it at night on trips to London and during the day driving a sawmill. This picture was taken at Roxton Park with early evening sunshine highlighting the working parts. During preservation it has had several owners, one of whom was the late Steve Neville, who travelled extensively with the *Duke of Kent*, usually with two Union Jack flags flying at the base of the chimney. Note also the hurricane lamp carried below the engine.

(Opposite, bottom) Two well-known 6 nhp Burrell road locomotives in action at the Great Dorset Steam Fair. Leading is Burrell *Duke of Kent* followed by 7 nhp no. 3057 *Lord Roberts*. This picture illustrates clearly many of the differences in the two designs.

Burrell road locomotive no. 3057 *Lord Roberts* is a fine example of the company's contractors' engine which were more heavily constructed than normal. It was completed in December 1908, and after many years on general haulage work it was eventually laid aside and in due course became derelict. It was very nearly sold for scrap but fortunately was rescued for preservation.

(Opposite, top) This splendid 5 nhp Burrell double-crank compound no. 3941 *The Badger* was turned out from Thetford in January 1923 in plum-coloured livery and was supplied to Major Hon. W.H. Pearson of Cowdrey Park, Midhurst, Sussex.

(Opposite, bottom) Road locomotives were very much in demand during the early 1900s. Burrell no. 3633 *Lord Kitchener* was completed in December 1914 and supplied new to W.E. Chivers & Sons of Devizes, Wiltshire. Burrells were well liked by this company, and over the years they operated several other Burrell road locomotives and wagons.

Several of the leading engine companies built road locomotives. Fowler engines were highly regarded for handling the heaviest loads. Burrells had long experience of building showmen's road locomotives, their engines all built to a similar style and lacking the showland glamour. Here, four powerful road locomotives stand coupled together, ready for a demonstration of their pulling power. Leading the line-up is Burrell no. 3257 *Clinker*; the other three are all Fowlers of varying types.

Wingham Agricultural Implement Co. Ltd of Wingham, Kent, took delivery of the 7 nhp Burrell road locomotive no. 3257 *Clinker* in early 1911, the engine having been completed in the January of that year. In the early 1920s it went to engine dealers Mornement & Ray of East Harling, Norfolk, ending its working life on fen drainage.

(Opposite, top) Several Burrell road locomotives now in preservation were formerly owned by J.H. Henton of Hopwas, Tamworth, Staffordshire. No. 3996 *Conqueror*, built in 1924, was supplied new to the Hentons, remaining with the family until 1976. The well-known Bostock & Wombwell showmen's road locomotives *Nero* and *Rajah* were also owned by Hentons, having been purchased at the Bostock auction held in November 1931 for £200 and £180 respectively.

(Opposite, bottom) Another Burrell road locomotive which was to end its working days with J.H. Henton of Hopwas was no. 3395 *City of Exeter*, later renamed *The Dalesman*. It was purchased by the Hentons in 1924 from its first owner, J. Hancock of Exeter, who used it on general haulage work. No. 3395 is a 6 nhp design completed in 1912.

This Burrell may be unfamiliar to some readers as it does not visit many events. No. 3777 *Queen Mary* was completed in December 1917 as a road locomotive and supplied to W.J. King of Bagborough, Taunton, Somerset, where it was used on brick and stone haulage. In 1948 it was laid aside and became derelict. Note the straked wheels and spoked flywheel fitted to this engine.

(Opposite, top) Burrell 6 nhp no. 3368 *Jellicoe* was built in 1912 and was to have several owners during its working life, the first being Hellier & Ellis of Chudleigh, Knighton, Devon. Seven years later it was bought by the East Down Threshing Company. It is currently preserved in Dorset.

(Opposite, bottom) Burrell 5 nhp no. 3917 *Triumph* was completed in 1921 and supplied to Thomas Podbury of Newton Poppleford, Devon. The road locomotive features were later additions.

Burrells completed this 5 nhp double-crank compound, no. 3824 *Lord Fisher of Lambeth*, in December 1919, and finished it in showman's colours for exhibition. After this it spent its entire working life with an owner in Somerset.

(Opposite, top) Burrell no. 3937 *Janet* was the last single-crank compound road locomotive built. It was supplied new to G. Birss of Crathes, Scotland, where it spent its entire working life, mostly hauling and powering portable stone-crushing equipment. It is currently preserved in Cornwall.

(Opposite, bottom) The Burrell single-crank compound 10 nhp no. 1876 *Emperor* photographed in 1965. It was built in 1895 as a showman's road locomotive for George Twigden of Leicester, and was later returned to Burrells where it was fitted with a crane and became the works engine. In 1929 *Emperor* passed into the ownership of engine dealers Mornement & Ray. During 1959 it was rescued for preservation from Stoke Ferry, restored, and attended a few events in East Anglia. In 1980 it was sold again and has since been restored as a showman's engine. It is now part of the Hollycombe Collection.

In the early 1960s Burrell crane engine no. 3829 *His Majesty* attended a few East Anglian rallies, albeit without its crane jib. It was still in the ownership of J. Hickey & Sons Ltd who used it for heavy haulage in the London area and later as works crane engine until it was laid aside. It was eventually restored to working order and, as mentioned, seen in public before being sold on in the early 1960s.

(Opposite, top) *His Majesty* photographed at an East Anglian rally in 1961, still in the ownership of J. Hickey & Sons Ltd. The nameplate can be seen mounted on the front of the cab.

(Opposite, bottom) This more recent picture of *His Majesty* shows the flywheel side of the engine which, as can be seen, is still on straked wheels. Completed in 1920, it was sold to T. & J.W. Cooper of Liskeard, Cornwall, being supplied as a crane engine without a jib. After only a few months it was sold on to J. Hickey & Sons where it was to remain for many years,

Burrell crane engine no. 3197 *Old Tim*. Built in 1910, it was sold to Screen Brothers of Oldbury, Birmingham. During the First World War pressure on the works was so great that the Burrell worked twenty-four hours a day, with double-manning. It continued working until 1958 when it went into very well-earned preservation. Remarkably, it was still in its original livery, despite its long and hard-working life.

(Opposite, top) Engine sales were already very low when Burrells built 5 nhp crane engine no. 4074 *The Lark* in 1927. It was sold to J. Reynolds of Bury St Edmunds in lake/red livery. This fine engine has been in preservation in Lincolnshire for many years, but only on rare occasions is it seen in public.

(Opposite, bottom) Preparation time at the Great Dorset Steam Fair as two Fowler crane engines, *Duke of York* and *Wolverhampton Wanderer*, assisted by Burrell single-crank compound no. 3937 *Janet*, get ready for another heavy haulage demonstration.

Foden 'Colonial' road locomotive no. 3534 *Monarch* was built in 1913 and was one of five originally intended for the overseas market. *Monarch* was the only one not sent abroad; instead it remained in Britain working on various duties. At one time it was with shipbuilders Cammell Laird, employed on haulage and winching work. Note the small belly tank fitted.

(Opposite, top) Due to their sheer size and the length of the crane jibs, crane engines are not the easiest subjects to photograph successfully. Fowler no. 17106 *Duke of York* is one of the best known of the big Fowlers, and it spent much of its working life with Marstons Road Services of Liverpool, hauling extremely heavy and awkward loads. One such load was the rudder of HMS *Ark Royal*, which weighed over 80 tons, and which *Duke of York* hauled from Darlington to Birkenhead.

(Opposite, bottom) This broadside view of Fowler no. 17106 *Duke of York*, this time without the jib fitted, certainly gives a true impression of the powerful B6 'Super Lion' design. These fine engines were capable of handling the heaviest loads, no easy job as visibility from the footplate was limited, and the length of the crane jib was often a hindrance.

This 7 nhp class A9 Fowler road locomotive, no. 14754 *Endeavour*, was completed in September 1920 and supplied new to the Essex-based company Drage & Kent, who used it on heavy haulage. Its working life was spent at a sawmill, from where it was rescued for preservation. After restoration by its new Suffolk-based owner, it appeared at a number of events in Eastern England. Several A9 class road locomotives are in preservation. This type of engine was also available as a single-cylinder version, and three examples were built between 1918 and 1920, but the compound version was more popular, with twenty being built in the same period. Most were for the home market, only one example going overseas.

A quiet moment at the Great Dorset Steam Fair for Fowler *Duke of York*, which was often referred to in its working days at Marstons Road Services as 'The Big Engine' – hardly an overstatement! The photograph illustrates the flywheel side with the jib in place.

(Opposite, top) Only a handful of Fowler crane engines have survived into preservation. This is the oldest: no. 8920 *The Great North* was built in 1901 and is a splendid example of the 8 nhp B5 class. It was supplied new to Stuart Dodds of Leith, and three years later the business was purchased by John Wilkinson. The Fowler continued to be worked by Wilkinson's until 1927 when it was laid aside. After thirty years it was repainted to celebrate the company's 110 years in business, after which it passed into preservation.

(Opposite, bottom) This is another view of *The Great North* taken at a northern rally while it was in preservation in County Durham. The crane hook has been securely fixed back to the jib to prevent it swinging free as the engine moves slowly round the main ring. Unlike some of the other crane engines, it is still on straked wheels, as it was in its working days. The various surviving crane engines have a fascination all their own, attracting much attention at events, particularly where demonstrations of the cranes in action are involved. The Fowler B6 class heavy haulage design was the ultimate crane engine.

A heavy load moves off at the Great Dorset Steam Fair. Burrell single-crank compound *Janet* leads the way, somewhat dwarfed by Fowler B6 'Super Lion' no. 17212 *Wolverhampton Wanderer*.

(Opposite, top) These two massive Fowler crane engines are of different designs. Nearest the camera is B6 no. 17212 *Wolverhampton Wanderer*, and alongside is the oldest surviving Fowler crane engine, B5 class no. 8920 *The Great North*, built twenty-eight years before.

(Opposite, bottom) In 1929 John Thompson of Ettingshall, Wolverhampton, took delivery of the massive Fowler B6 class crane engine no. 17212 *Wolverhampton Wanderer*. It was soon set to work delivering Lancashire-type boilers all over the country, a job it continued to do until 1948 when it became the works engine.

Fowler A9 class road locomotive no. 15649 *Providence* was built in 1920. In 1966 this engine became famous for hauling the new 15-inch gauge railway locomotive *River Mite* from York to Ravenglass, Cumbria, a long and difficult journey across the Pennines.

(Opposite, top) The flywheel side of *Providence*. The lettering, which is just visible between the front wheels, reads 'Age shall not weary them'.

(Opposite, bottom) Several A9 class 7 nhp road locomotives that were built just after the First World War have survived. They include no. 15649 *Providence*, seen here quietly moving round the main ring.

With a large caterpillar tractor in tow, Fowler *Pride of Wales* and McLaren *Boadicea* open up to tackle the hilly section at the Great Dorset Steam Fair. The leading engine, Fowler no. 8712, is one of the oldest surviving Fowler road locomotives, built at Leeds in 1900.

The 1996 Great Dorset Steam Fair saw a magnificent collection of Fowler-built engines, ranging from showmen's road locomotives to steamrollers. A9 class 7 nhp no. 15462 *Ajax* was built in 1919 and supplied new to Packers of Cheltenham. Its second owners were based in North Yorkshire where it was used on agricultural haulage work. In 1959 it passed into preservation and still remains in the county.

This Fowler 7 nhp compound road locomotive is class A7 no. 13141 *Jo*, which was completed in September 1913. It is one of only two road engines of this type to survive in the British Isles. It spent its final working years on agricultural work during the Second World War, first for the Hampshire War Agricultural Committee and later in Yorkshire.

Many showmen's and heavy haulage engines ended their working days on agricultural work. One such was Fowler 7 nhp class A8 no. 14100 *Empress*, which worked until the mid-1960s. This engine was completed in July 1914 and supplied to M. Wakefield of Houghton-le-Spring, County Durham, for general haulage work.

The flywheel side of *Empress*. This splendid Fowler was not sold into preservation until 1984 and is currently to be found in Yorkshire.

Fowler class A9 no. 15467 *Sir Douglas* was built in 1920 and returned to the rally field in 1996 after a long absence, having undergone a complete rebuild. Only a few A9 class road engines have survived.

Fowler B6 class no. 14115 *The Lion* was built in December 1914 and was supplied to the War Department, seeing service in France during most of the First World War. In 1921 it was sold to London & Kentish Haulage and was later taken over by Pickfords. Its final working years were spent in the Manchester area until it was laid up in 1946, eventually becoming derelict. Many long hours of restoration work have resulted in the fine engine we see today.

For nearly thirty years this Fowler 7 nhp class A9 road locomotive stood on Cardiff Docks. No. 15463 *Dreadnought* was supplied new to Robert Wynn & Sons, haulage contractors of Newport, in 1920, and remained in their ownership for the rest of its short working life. *Dreadnought* was rescued and rebuilt to celebrate the company's centenary in 1963, after which it again went into storage until sold for preservation.

(Opposite, top) This Fowler class A9 road locomotive was a familiar sight at early rallies carrying the name *Belle of the Wolds*, being preserved at Bridlington. It subsequently disappeared from view for eighteen years until a complete rebuild by new owners returned it to the rally fields. It now carries the name *Ajax*.

(Opposite, bottom) Fowler D5 class compound three-speed road locomotive no. 19338 *Monty* was completed in February 1931. Its early working life was spent on an estate where it was used to haul timber and to provide power to machinery.

This superbly restored Fowler road locomotive is class A4 no. 9456 *Jess*, completed in August 1902. It is one of only a very small number of this type of road engine to survive. It was supplied new to R. Cann of Wareham, Dorset, and later sold to an owner in East Peckham. *Jess* was later to enter showland service, travelling with Sussex-based owner T. Smith in the southern counties.

(Opposite, top) This Fowler R3 class road engine was ordered by the War Department but it was not completed until a month after the First World War had finished. No. 15323 *Excelsior* was to spend much of its working life in Derbyshire, eventually going for scrap in the late 1940s. Fortunately it was rescued for preservation and has now been with its current owner for nearly thirty years.

(Opposite, bottom) Fowler B6 no. 12226 *Titan* was built at Leeds in 1911. (This engine should not be confused with the earlier B6 of the same name which was employed on heavy haulage by Edward Box & Son.) The B6 design was widely used for all types of haulage work. Note the unusual wooden block tyres fitted to this engine. It worked at Spurr Inmans boiler works before being sold to a scrapyard, from where it was rescued for preservation.

One of the best known of all surviving road locomotives is Fowler no. 1705 *Atlas* which was built in 1928 and supplied new to Norman E. Box. This company operated a fleet of Fowlers at one time, and they were responsible for hauling a great many heavy and often difficult loads throughout the British Isles. *Atlas* is the only survivor of the fleet.

(Opposite, top) These two superb Fowler B6 class road locomotives thrilled the crowds at the Great Dorset Steam Fair with a heavy haulage demonstration. In their working days both these engines were used on the heaviest haulage work. The lead engine is no. 1705 *Atlas*, once operated by Norman E. Box. No. 1706 *Duke of York*, seen here without jib and fittings, was owned by Marston Road Services. They were completed at Leeds in May and July 1928 respectively.

(Opposite, bottom) This photograph shows the two Fowlers arriving at the 25th Great Dorset Steam Fair in 1993. The road train had attracted much attention on its way to the show, especially when tackling the numerous inclines on the way.

Seventy-five TE2 haulage and winding engines were ordered by the Ministry of Munitions in 1917. After the war all were sold off at low prices, seriously depressing the market for several years. One of these engines, Fowler no. 14925 *Windrush*, is currently preserved at Marknesse, Holland. It is a splendid example of Fowler's TE2 design. This picture was taken in 1993, immediately after restoration in Britain was completed. Note the winding drum mounted beneath the boiler.

Fowler A7 no. 13141 *Jo*. Many of these haulage engines appeared in their working days with straked wheels, clean and smart but not overdecorated. Fowlers of Leeds were involved with many types of steam power, including railway locomotives, but they will always be remembered for their powerful road locomotives and ploughing engines.

(Opposite, top) The Fowler TE2 haulage winding engines were widely known as 'Russian Fowlers', after a considerable order for them was placed by the Russian military authorities. When the contract was subsequently cancelled, some were used by the British Army or bought by private customers. No. 14933 *Challenger* spent much of its working life near Sleaford in Lincolnshire, being purchased for preservation over fifty years ago.

(Opposite, bottom) At the Great Dorset Steam Fair there is an area especially set aside for the popular heavy haulage engine demonstrations. Here Fowler *Pride of Wales* and McLaren *Boadicea* get to grips with the climb to the top of the site with a large caterpillar tractor in tow. Such demonstrations give the owners of these powerful engines a rare opportunity to haul heavy loads over hilly terrain, requiring the engines to work hard.

Only a few 5 nhp Fowler type D2 road locomotives are in preservation. No. 12899 *Western Star* was completed in 1912 and supplied to Carmarthen County Council. Its duties included stone haulage. Ten years later it was sold to a contractor who used it for threshing and driving a sawmill.

(Opposite, top) Fowler A4 class no. 8712 *Pride of Wales* was built in 1900 and supplied new to J.H. & R.O. Morse, haulage contractors of Norbeth, Pembrokeshire. Looking at this picture it is difficult to believe that it spent many years in the open, eventually becoming derelict. The superb engine we see today is the result of a long, careful restoration project. It is one of the oldest Fowler road locomotives in existence.

(Opposite, bottom) This snatched shot of two Fowlers, *Pride of Wales* and *Duke of York*, working hard at the top of the climb at the Great Dorset Steam Fair conveys well the thrilling spectacle that these demonstrations provide.

This Fowler road engine, A7 class no. 13138 *Finella*, is currently preserved in Aberdeen and is seldom seen south of the border. Built in 1914, it was supplied new to Mr J. Sherris, threshing contractor of Auchinblac, Aberdeenshire. In 1942 it changed hands and was then principally used on timber work.

(Opposite, top) Some engines seen at early rallies looked very different from today. This is Fowler no. 15323 *Excelsior*, pictured at Rempstone in 1963. Compare this with the picture on page 123. Among other changes, the overall length canopy had been replaced.

(Opposite, bottom) Fowler class D2 no. 12693 *Brunel*, built in 1911. This photograph was taken at Truthwall, St Just, Cornwall, over thirty years ago. It is still to be found in the same county. The oldest surviving D2 road locomotive in Britain was built in 1909, although examples of this class in traction and road roller form built in the late nineteenth century have also survived.

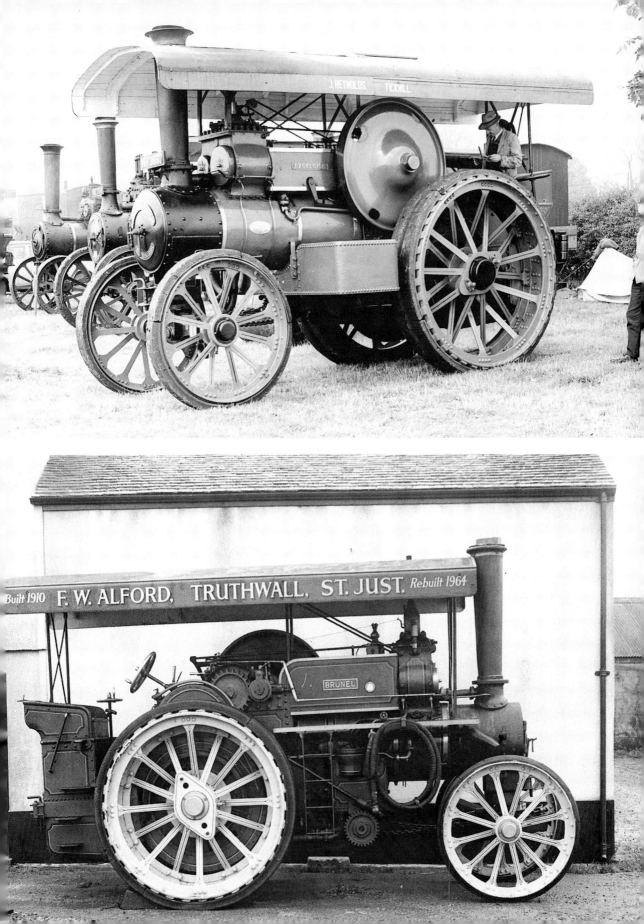

Resplendent in War Department livery, this is Fowler type TE2 haulage and winding engine no. 14950, pictured in the late 1960s at Hinchingbrooke Park, Huntingdon. Built in 1918, it was originally ordered by the Ministry of Munitions and was sold after the war. These Fowlers, with their dual capabilities, were also generally regarded as a powerful haulage engine.

(Opposite, top) Fowler B5 no. 8903 *Lord Roberts*, built in 1900. This engine was supplied new to Market Lavington brickworks and was principally used for brick haulage. At the time this photograph was taken, over thirty years ago, it was part of the famous Holywell collection which was auctioned in 1980.

(Opposite, bottom) Only a small number of road engines passed straight into preservation when their working life finished, but this was the case with Garrett 6 nhp compound road locomotive no. 27946 *Vera*. Built in 1909, it was supplied new to J. Harkness of Belfast where it remained in use for fifty-eight years, setting the record for the longest period of service by any road locomotive in the British Isles.

Fifty-five of these powerful 10 nhp McLaren road locomotives were built for the War Department during the First World War for hauling 49mm guns. No. 1652 *Boadicea* was completed in 1919, after the war had finished, and was thus never sent to France. Eventually, along with many other wagons and engines, it was sold to a private owner and used on heavy haulage. In due course it again changed hands, this time to Edward Corrigan, a Filey-based showman, and was converted to full showman's specification with the name *Gigantic*. It was found to be too heavy and was resold and used by the new owners for general haulage. Its last work was on fenland dredging before it was laid up in 1958.

(Opposite, top) The McLaren *Boadicea* appears at many events across the country throughout the year. Here it is in action at Parham, Sussex.

(Opposite, bottom) This picture of *Boadicea* was taken many years ago when it was in the ownership of the late Steve Neville who purchased it for preservation. As it was still in good condition, he lit the fire and drove it the 80 miles to its new home. Over the years *Boadicea* became a familiar sight on the highways, often travelling considerable distances to and from events. In 1965 Steve Neville sold the engine after purchasing a Burrell showman's.

The McLaren 10 nhp design was among the engines chosen by the War Department for use in the First World War, in this case for hauling guns. Three 10 nhp engines are in preservation in this country, two of which were originally built for the War Department. The third, built in 1912, went overseas, and returned to England from Australia several years ago. This picture shows the flywheel side of *Boadicea* in recent years. Late afternoon sunshine highlights the polished brass and gleaming paintwork. Note the twisted brasswork at the front of the canopy.

Another McLaren road locomotive that has been in preservation for many years is 8 nhp no. 1421 *Captain Scott*. Built in 1913, it was supplied new to Whitlocks of Conisborough, Yorkshire, where it was used in their quarry and for stone haulage. In 1914 it was commandeered by the War Department and used on airfield construction.

(Opposite, top) Another picture of McLaren *Captain Scott* showing the spoked flywheel. After wartime service in 1918, the engine was sold to a new owner at Barton on Humber, this time for general haulage. Its final working days were spent near Chesterfield and it was laid aside in 1945. Ten years later it was rescued for preservation, and its first rally appearance came in 1956.

(Opposite, bottom) McLarens of Leeds, like many other engine builders, built up a lucrative export market. No. 1332, a 10 nhp engine, was built in 1912 and sent to Australia, where it spent its working life. It eventually returned to this country for preservation, since when it has had several owners. It is currently undergoing a complete overhaul.

4. Steam Tractors

During the First World War many tractors were built for the War Department, while others were requisitioned. After the war ended the War Stores Disposal Board was set up to sell off many thousands of items including steam tractors and wagons. Their condition varied greatly: some had been hardly used while others were in a very poor condition or worn out. It was possible to pick up numerous bargains at a fraction of the cost of a new unit. All were quickly snapped up by both companies and private individuals, and such was the demand at the time that tractor building actually increased. But, even if it was not readily apparent at the time, the writing was on the wall as the motor lorry was already on the scene and by the mid-1920s the demand for new tractors had dwindled to very small numbers. In preservation today are a considerable number of tractors which spent their early years in government service, including several examples of the popular Garrett 4CD design. Steam tractors were versatile and used for many types of work, such as stone haulage, furniture removal, and transporting market garden produce. For many years they were supplied on straked wheels, and the arrival of solid rubber tyres must have been very popular with enginemen, giving them a much more comfortable ride. Most engine building companies were involved in the tractor market, and in preservation today are examples of many different designs.

Aveling & Porter are best known for their steamrollers, which were sold in considerable numbers both in Britain and overseas. The company also built many other types of steam engine, including steam tractors, which they produced over a long period. This is 4 nhp GND class tractor no. 8288 *Fire Queen*, built in 1914. It is seen here towing a Farmers Foundry Co. portable engine at the Huntingdonshire County Show in the early 1960s. At the time it was part of a sizeable collection based at Holywell near St Ives.

(Opposite, top) Built in 1920, this Aveling & Porter 4 nhp KND class tractor no. 9225 *Clementine* was sold to Hereford County Council. It had a long working life and was not retired until 1955. It is seen here in very dusty conditions hauling timber.

(Opposite, bottom) This Aveling & Porter 4 nhp type XAC no. 6319 *Queen of Herts* is an example of the company's convertible design, built in 1907. It has been on the rally fields in tractor form since the early 1990s.

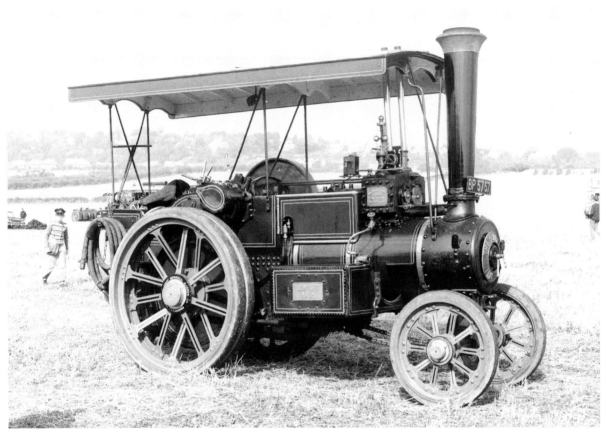

Burrell 'Gold Medal' tractor no. 3815 *Sunset No. 2* photographed at Winchester in 1967. Built in 1919, it was supplied new to A.E. Johnson of Pulborough, Sussex, and used principally for timber haulage work. It is now part of the Hollycombe collection.

(Opposite, top) Burrell no. 3626 *Jane Eyre* was completed in October 1914 and supplied to H. Hickan & Son of Princes Risborough. Just two years later it was commandeered by the War Department, along with many other engines and wagons. After the war it spent some time in showland ownership.

(Opposite, bottom) In their early years, Fodens built traction engines and road locomotives, examples of which have survived into preservation. In due course they began to concentrate purely on wagons and steam tractors. Only three of these Foden 'Sun' tractors, officially known as the M type, were constructed. Two were exported but no. 13730, built in 1930, remained in this country. Another has since returned from South Africa. This picture was taken in the 1960s at one of the famous Woburn rallies.

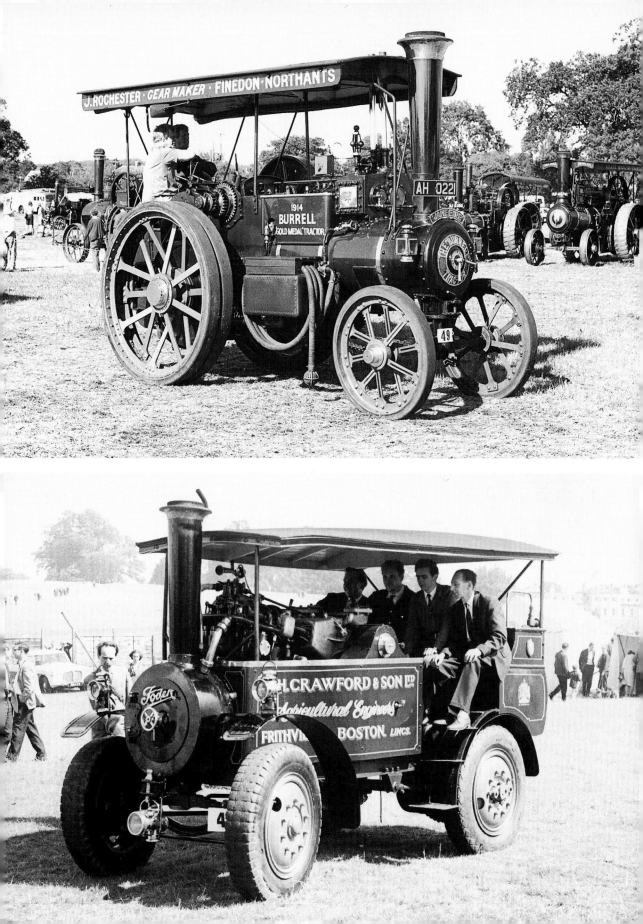

Another early rally picture, this is Burrell 'Gold Medal' tractor no. 4072 *Tinkerbell*, pictured at Ickleton in 1962. This tractor was completed at Thetford in August 1927 and sold to Stemp & Weller of Cranleigh, Surrey, for timber work.

(Opposite, top) This is a recent picture of Burrell 4 nhp no. 4072 *Tinkerbell*, with the name of its first owner on the engine canopy. Fortunately a considerable number of 'Gold Medal' tractors have survived into preservation.

(Opposite, bottom) The Burrell tractor *Tinkerbell* in action at Weeting with a heavy traction wagon in tow. Several of these very versatile 'Gold Medal' tractors were present at this event, some having travelled a considerable distance. Tractor sales in the late 1920s were at a low ebb, and only one 'younger' Burrell tractor from this period has survived – no. 4084, built three months after *Tinkerbell*. This 'Gold Medal' tractor is currently based at the Museum of Science and Industry in Birmingham.

Foden tractor no. 13222 *Cheshire Maid* was built in 1928 and its first owner was S. Darke & Son of Worcester. It later passed into the ownership of F.H. Grover of Amersham, Buckinghamshire, and in due course went on to Mr Noble, a showman based in County Durham. Its final working years were spent threshing for J. Hugill of Brompton-on-Swale, Yorkshire. Until about 1959 this tractor was on solid rubber tyres.

(Opposite, top) Built in 1928, Foden no. 13196 was supplied new to the Atlas Transport & Shipping Co. Ltd of Chiswick and later sold to Q.M. Cameroux & Co. Ltd of Fulham, where it acquired the name *Pride of Fulham*. During the 1960s it was a familiar sight at events in the Midlands. After many years out of public view it made a very welcome reappearance a few years ago.

(Opposite, bottom) Foden D Type tractor no. 13068 *Perseverance* was built in 1928 and, like so many other tractors of various types, it spent its early working years on timber haulage in the ownership of A.L. Watkins of Brecon, South Wales. It was later sold to Langley & Johnson of Slough. During the war it was owned by London County Council's War Debris Committee and was used to demolish bombed buildings in London. In due course it was sold to Hardwicks from where it was rescued for preservation.

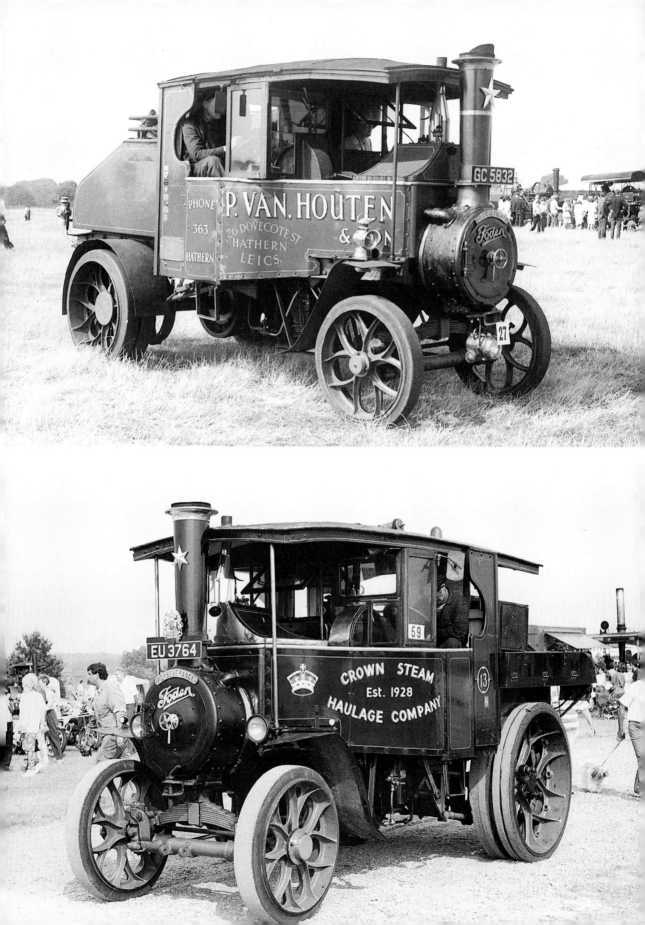

This Foden was to have a very short working life of just fifteen years. Built in 1933 as works no. 14084, it was supplied new to J. Murch of Umberleigh, Devon. It was to have two more owners before being laid aside in 1948. The youngest surviving Foden in the British Isles, it was rescued in the early 1950s for preservation.

(Opposite, top) Much of this Foden tractor's working life was spent in the London Docks with its first owner, Beck & Pollitzer, operating with a low trailer from the company's Lambeth depot. It was fitted with pneumatic tyres and lighting in the 1930s. In 1944 it was sold to a new owner and eventually laid aside, being rescued for preservation in 1975. Restoration took five years to complete.

(Opposite, bottom) This Foden has an interesting history. It was completed in 1926 as an experimental half-track, works no. 12300. It was rebuilt in 1930 as a conventional tractor, works no. 13484. It is seen here complete with a timber wagon at Bedfordshire Steam and Country Fair.

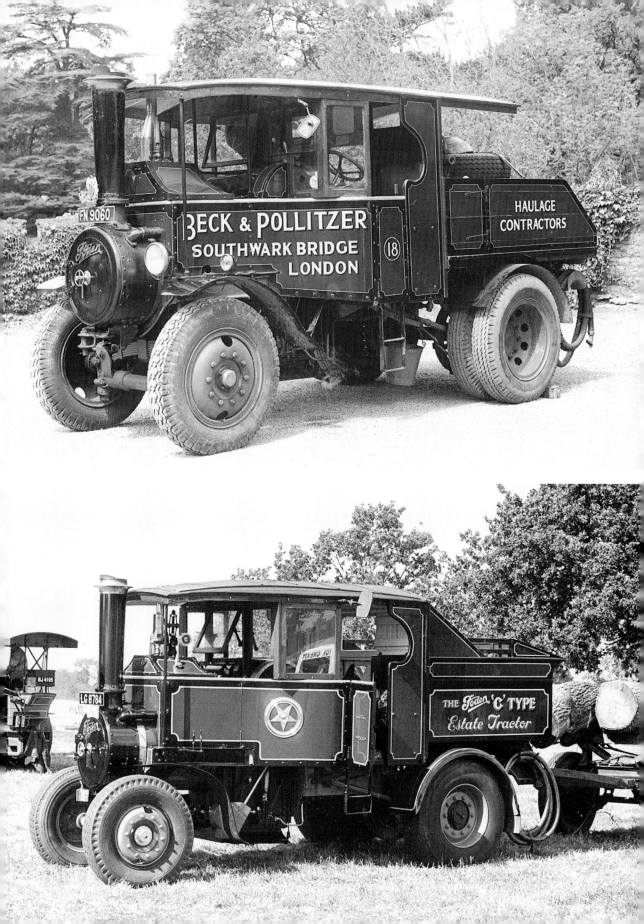

Foden no. 14084 *Duchess* photographed in 1998 shortly after changing ownership and moving to the north of England. The tractor is on solid rubber tyres.

(Opposite, top) Fowler 'Tiger' tractor no. 14406 *Mtoto* was built at Leeds in 1917 and supplied to G.D. Best of Canon Pyon, Herefordshire, later passing to another owner in the same county, C. & J. Smith of Pencombe. In the mid-1940s it was sold to its last commercial owner in Shropshire. Some readers may recall this engine by its earlier name of *Pandora*.

(Opposite, bottom) In the early 1960s two very large traction engine rallies were held at Raynham Hall near Fakenham in Norfolk, with engines from far and wide on display, and crowds of visitors. This picture of Garrett 4CD no. 38818 *Wendy*, built in 1920, was taken there; at the time the engine was preserved at Wickham Market.

Engine names often change in preservation. Garrett 4CD no. 33295 *Princess Alexandra* is seen here at Rempstone in the 1960s, when it was in preservation at Bridlington. This engine was one of a large batch built for the War Department during the First World War. By the time it was completed in May 1918, the war was almost over.

(Opposite, top) Garrett no. 33295 again, this time carrying the name *Princess Royal*. This engine still carries the twisted brass that dates back to its fairground days with Henry Thurston when it was named *Felix*. This engine has not been seen in public for several years as it is currently awaiting overhaul.

(Opposite, bottom) Garretts built a considerable number of their popular 4CD tractors for the War Department, including no. 33278 *Princess Mary*, completed in May 1918. In 1922 it was purchased by Mr Jarvis, who was based at Heath Hayes near Birmingham, and it was converted to showman's specification, hauling and powering a bioscope show. Its final working days were spent on general haulage work based at Wolverhampton. In preservation it has had several owners.

Over five hundred of these Garrett 4CDs were built. No. 31633 *Mr Potter* was completed in March 1913 and supplied to Ephraim Clarke of Hadleigh. Two years later it moved to T. & A.J. Mann, timber hauliers of Earls Colne, and after one more owner it was sold to W.C. French. In preservation the engine required many new parts, having stood in a playground for several years after its working days were over. The majority of the 4CD tractors in preservation have a longer canopy and thus look very different. No. 31633 *Mr Potter* is seen here at a Weeting Rally, a major event in the traction engine calendar, held every July near Brandon.

159

Garrett no. 33380 was a typical 4CD tractor when this picture was taken at Ickleton in 1962. Built in 1918, it was among those supplied to the War Department. After changing hands, it was converted into a showman's tractor and named *Sapphire*. The 4CD tractor was Garrett's most successful design, with 514 examples built over a 21-year period. It was available as Standard and Colonial models, and could also be used as a steamroller. Fortunately, a large number have survived into preservation.

(Opposite, top) Another of the 4CD Garrett tractors built in 1918 for the War Department was no. 33141 *Julie*, which saw service in France. Most of the engine's later life was spent on agricultural work. It still carries twisted brass canopy supports.

(Opposite, bottom) Garrett 4CD no. 33632 *Joyce*, completed in September 1919, awaits the day's events at Harewood House in 1964. When this engine was built the market was already flooded with surplus engines and wagons that were sold off following the end of the First World War.

A splendid example of the 4CD class, no. 33991 *Patricia* was built in 1921 and supplied new to Martley District Council. Its final working years were spent on timber haulage. It has been a familiar sight at engine rallies for many years.

(Opposite, top) The Garrett 4CD was one of the most successful small tractor designs, ideal for light haulage and threshing work and well liked by those who worked them. No. 34539 *Evelyn* was built in 1924, going new to W. Bailey of Hengrave, Suffolk, where it was to remain for fifteen years. It changed hands in 1939 and was in use for a further seven years.

(Opposite, bottom) Production of the famous 4CD tractor was nearing its end when no. 34641 *Bunty* was built in 1925, although it continued for a further four years. This engine was exhibited at the prestigious Smithfield Show before going to its first owner, Clare Rural District Council. It has been part of the Bressingham Collection for many years.

The last of a long line of 4CD tractors was no. 35225, completed on 2 September 1929. Fortunately it has survived. When this engine was built, tractor sales were at a very low ebb.

(Opposite, top) Very few Garrett 'Suffolk Punch' tractors were built, of which only this one, no. 33180 *The Joker*, has survived. These were principally intended to counter the increasing flow of internal combustion engine tractors coming on to the market. Despite being a well thought out, if somewhat unconventional, design, it did not catch on. *The Joker* is now to be found at the Garrett Museum, Leiston.

(Opposite, bottom) Only a small number of engines built by the Mann Patent Steam Cart & Wagon Co. Ltd of Leeds have survived. No. 1325 *Myfanwy* was built in 1918 and supplied to a farming co-operative on Anglesey. It spent its working life on a variety of work, including haulage, wood sawing and threshing.

Only three tractors built by McLarens, another of the Leeds-based engine builders, are in preservation in the British Isles. No. 1837 *Bluebell*, completed in April 1936, was used for timber haulage in the west country and later at Southampton Docks. It has been in preservation for a great many years, travelling many miles under its own steam to events, often towing Garrett 4CD no. 33380 *Sapphire*.

Ransomes, Sims & Jefferies, one of the East Anglian-based engine building companies, were best known for their very good traction engines. Despite Garretts being in the same county, they also built tractors. No. 39149, completed in October 1928, is the youngest of the handful of survivors.

(Opposite, top) This 4 nhp Ransomes, Sims & Jefferies tractor was supplied new to a Sussex-based builders merchants, and spent its early days moving building materials and general haulage. No. 39127 *General Wolfe* was completed in September 1928.

(Opposite, bottom) Only nine of these Robey 'Express' tractors were built, two of which have survived. The 'Express' was a rather unconventional design, with both coal and water stored behind the driver. No. 43388's last commercial owner was W. Smith's Sawmills of Fakenham, Norfolk. No. 43388 was completed in February 1929. The other surviving example is two years older. Robey & Co. Ltd, of the Globe Works, Lincoln, was one of four major traction engine companies based in that city. Another company, Marshalls, was based in Gainsborough, not far away. All five built steam tractors.

Sentinel timber tractor no. 8777 *Old Bill* is a DG4 design built in 1933. It was supplied new to Judds of Spencers Wood near Reading for timber haulage throughout the country. Its last commercial owner was in Shropshire. These were powerful tractors of which only four examples survive.

(Opposite, top) In all there are five Robey tractors in preservation in the British Isles, the two 'Expresses' mentioned earlier and three of conventional design. No. 33957 *Village Queen* is the oldest; built in 1915, it was supplied new to Fisher & Co. of Tamworth.

(Opposite, bottom) Sentinel tractor no. 7527, built in 1928, photographed at one of the Raynham events in the early 1960s. This tractor is now in preservation in Holland.

This rather unusual Sentinel 'Super' tractor spent its entire working life in the ownership of Teignmouth Quay Co., shunting railway wagons, a duty it performed until the early 1960s. Works no. 5644 *The Elephant* was built in 1924, and was one of a pair originally ordered by Sentinel's Calcutta agent but never sent. It has had several owners in preservation, including one in Holland.

(Opposite, top) Only a few of these powerful Sentinel timber tractors were constructed, mainly because of the high costs. DG4 design no. 8756 *Brutus* was built in 1933 and supplied to T. Place & Sons Ltd of Northallerton. It was to have several other owners before passing into preservation. It is now on display at Bressingham Steam Museum.

(Opposite, bottom) Sentinel no. 5558 started life as a wagon, leaving the works in 1924 for its first owners Hodgesons Brewery of Kingston upon Thames, working on beer deliveries in London. In the early 1930s it was bought by Symonds, Hunt & Montgomery Ltd of Liverpool. Not long afterwards it was sent to the Sentinel service garage and converted into a tractor. It was one of a number that were rebuilt, of which only three survive. No. 5559 continued working in the ownership of Criddle & Co. of Liverpool until 1962.

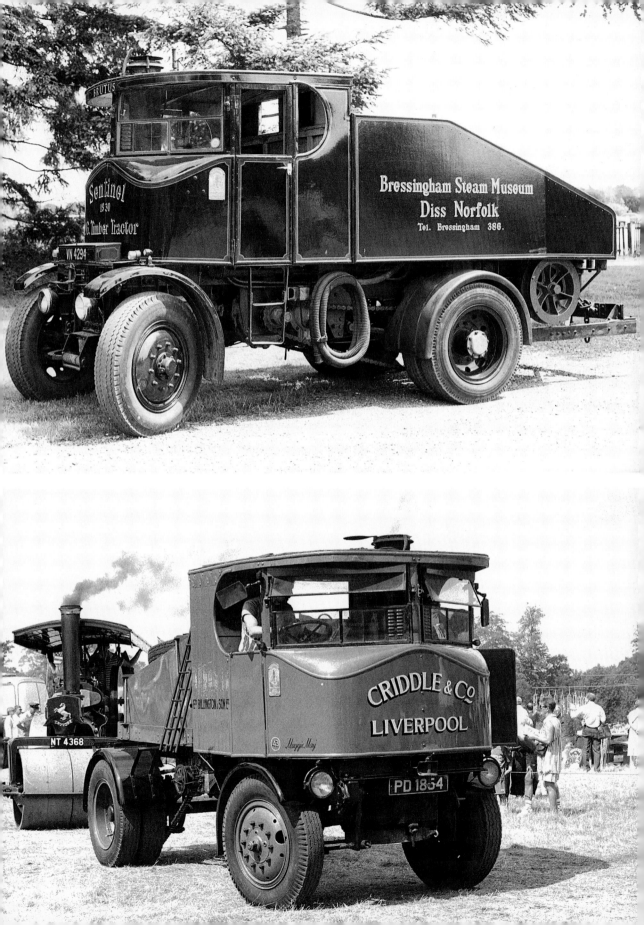

Another of the surviving DG4 tractors is no. 9097, built in 1934 and supplied to A. Woolton & Sons of Cannock, Staffordshire, later passing to C. James & Son of Kingswinford. It is seen here in rather heavy going at the Great Dorset Steam Fair. The winch mounted at the rear can easily be seen.

(Opposite, top) This sturdy Tasker 'Little Giant' tractor, no. 1895, was completed in 1922. It is a class B2 5 nhp compound slide-valve three-speed engine. Notice the highly polished brass maker's plate near the footplate.

(Opposite, bottom) This typical Wallis & Steevens tractor, no. 7871, was photographed at Raynham Hall in 1962. It is an example of the company's oil-bath 4 nhp compound design built in 1926. The two Raynham events of 1962 and 1963 were the largest to be held in the area at the time, drawing huge crowds daily; they are well remembered by enginemen and enthusiasts. Wallis & Steevens were also heavily involved with steamroller production, introducing their successful 'Advance' design, with its high-pressure cylinders and piston valves, after the First World War, principally for the newer road surfaces being developed at the time.

Several examples of the Wallis &
Steevens oil-bath tractor designs still
survive. No. 7641 *Gunner*, built in 1920,
is a fine example. The features of this
neat, compact 4 nhp design can be
clearly seen in this picture. Engines of
this type were especially popular with
market gardeners. The company also
offered a smaller 3 nhp design, the
earliest surviving example being
completed in 1902. These small engines
were often to be found at large country
houses, where they were used to
convey coal and other materials to the
estate from the local railway station.

176

Showmen's road locomotives in their working days hauled huge loads of up to eight wagons around the country. Narrow roads, steep gradients and varying road surfaces were all taken in their stride. On arrival at the fairground site, which was most likely a grassed area, moving the wagons into position required great skill, often in wet greasy conditions: all very different from conditions in this picture of *The Busy Bee* as it trundles along to Roxton Rally with a very light load.